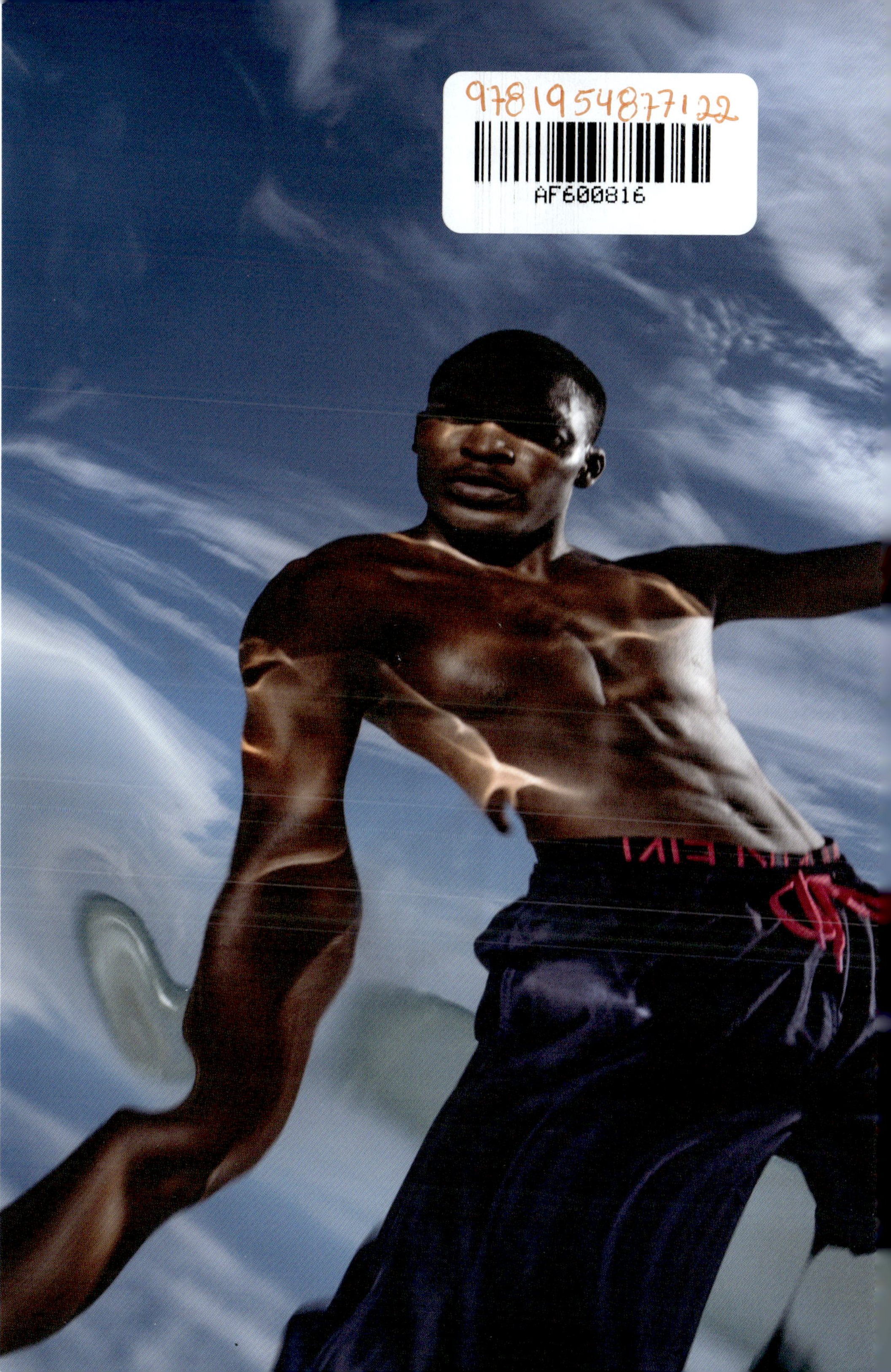

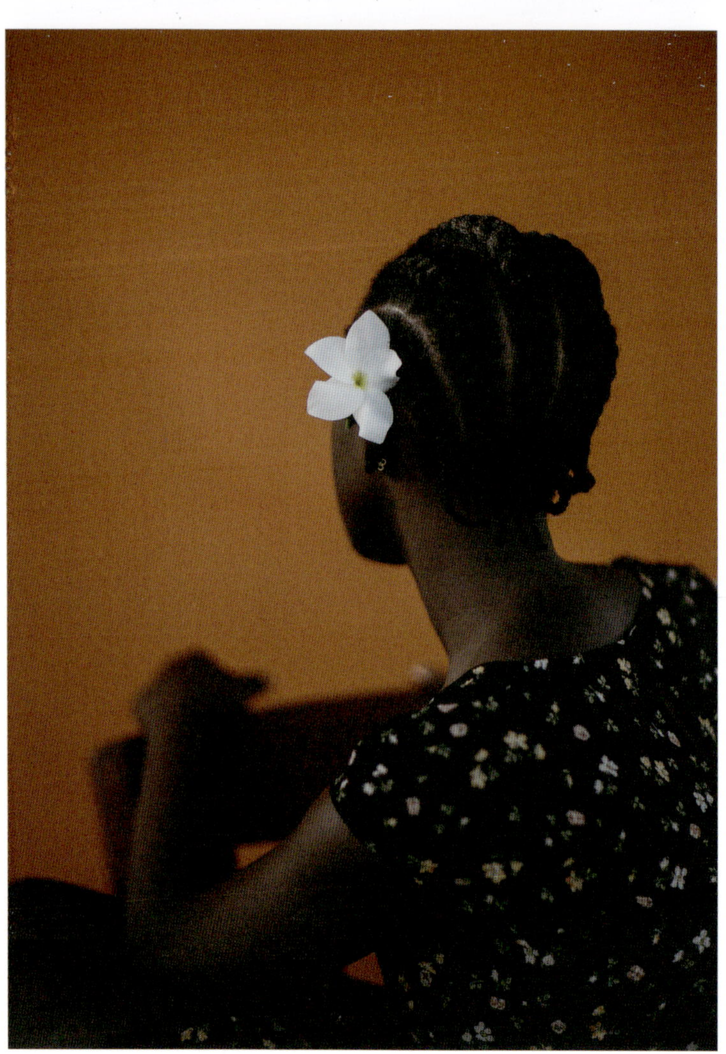

The Bahamas has suffered a lot in the past couple of years—enduring the aftermath and unfathomable devastation of Hurricane Dorian and then receiving another massive blow, that was the Covid-19 pandemic shortly after.

As an artist whose creations at the time were totally reliant upon my interactions with Bahamians in the everyday, to say that this time had been difficult for me would be an understatement. But with the introduction of safety protocols and vaccines, I was able to adjust my process and continue to create images.

The circumstances that led to the majority of these images was pure happenstance, which is usually a big part of my process when working in The Bahamas. I ready myself and remain open to the possibilities. I'm always inspired by the people who I photograph, their stories and connections to their landscapes. I feel that there's so much to be learned, about yourself and others, if you're willing to hold space for another and observe.

+ Melissa Alcena

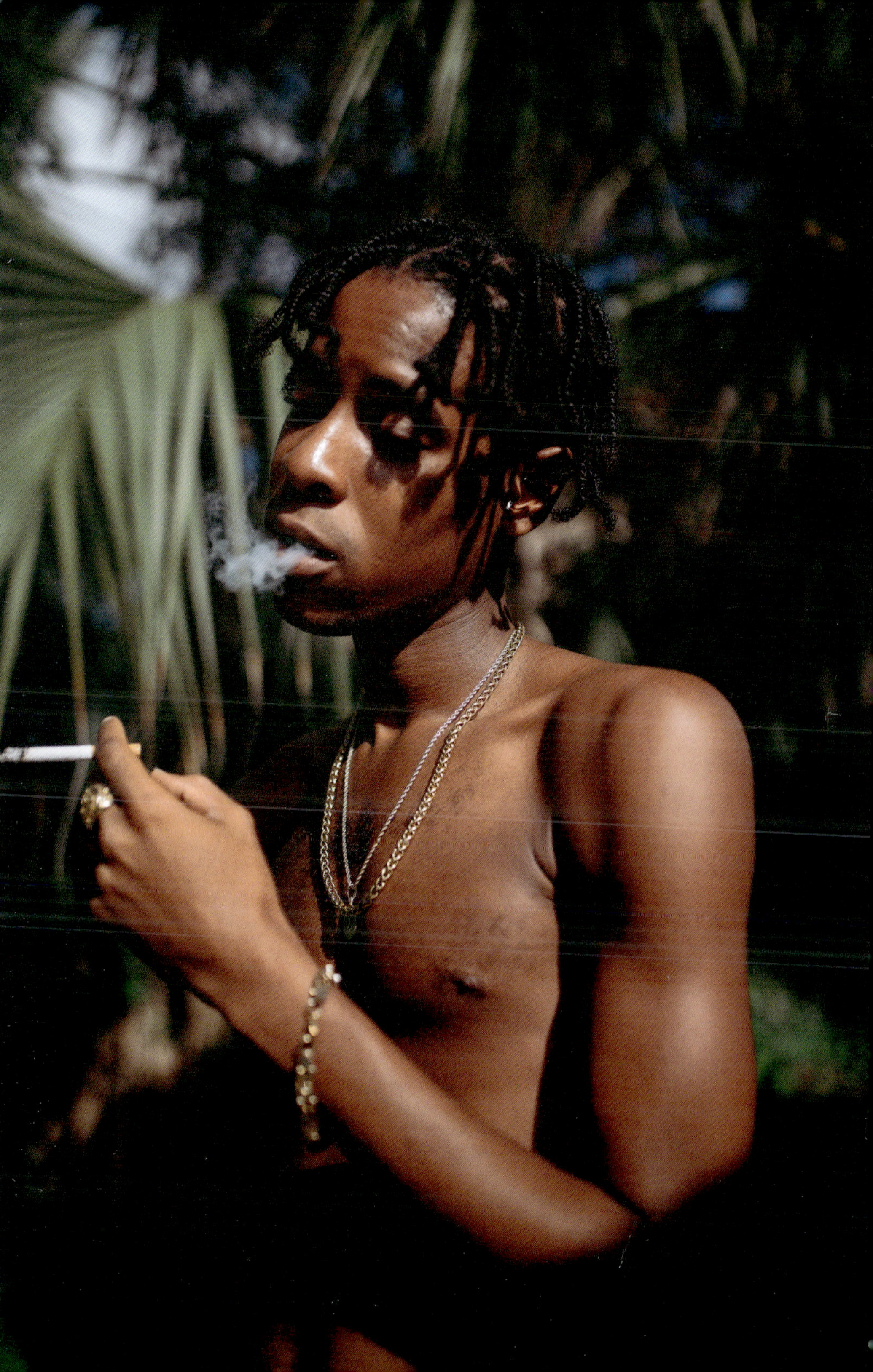

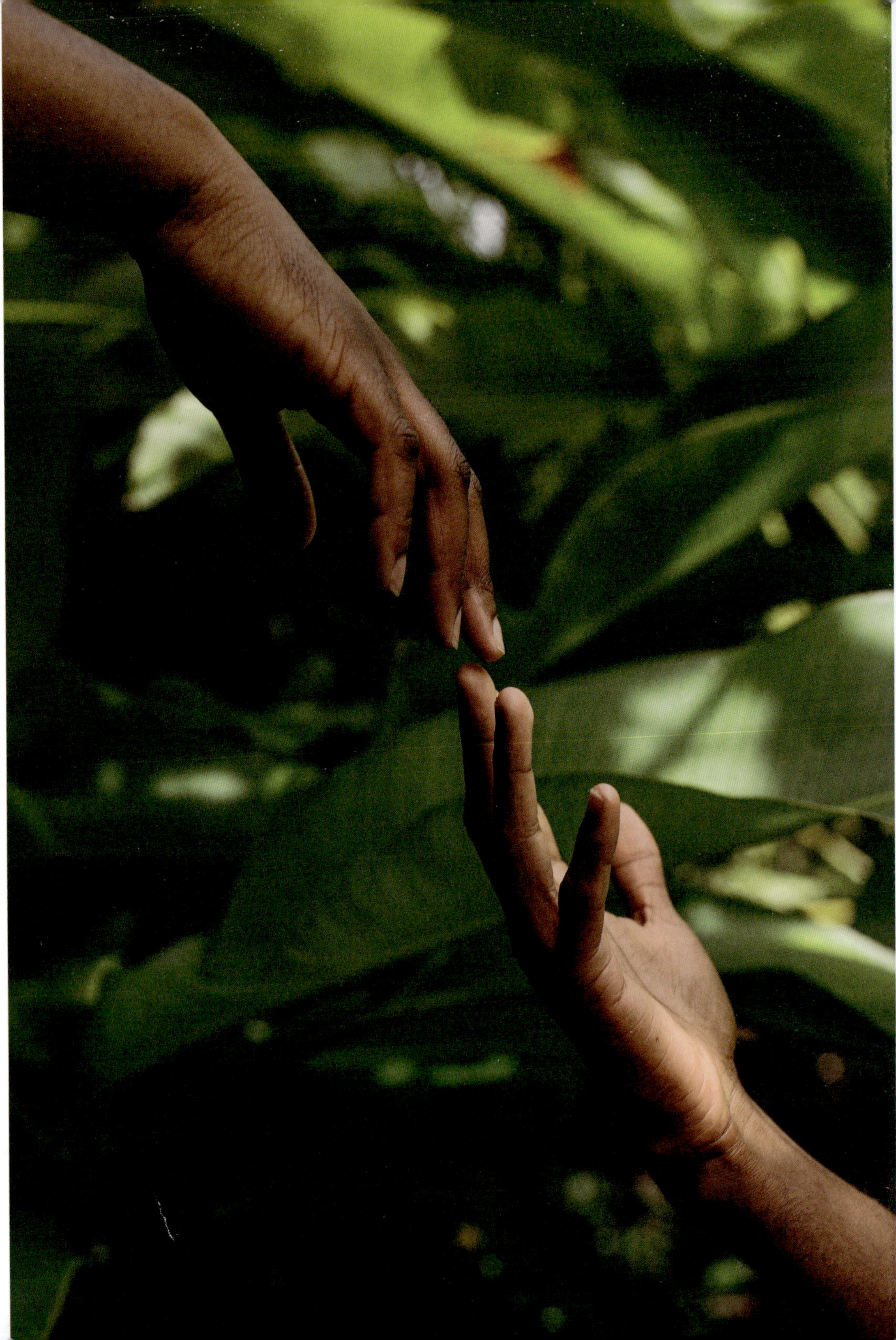

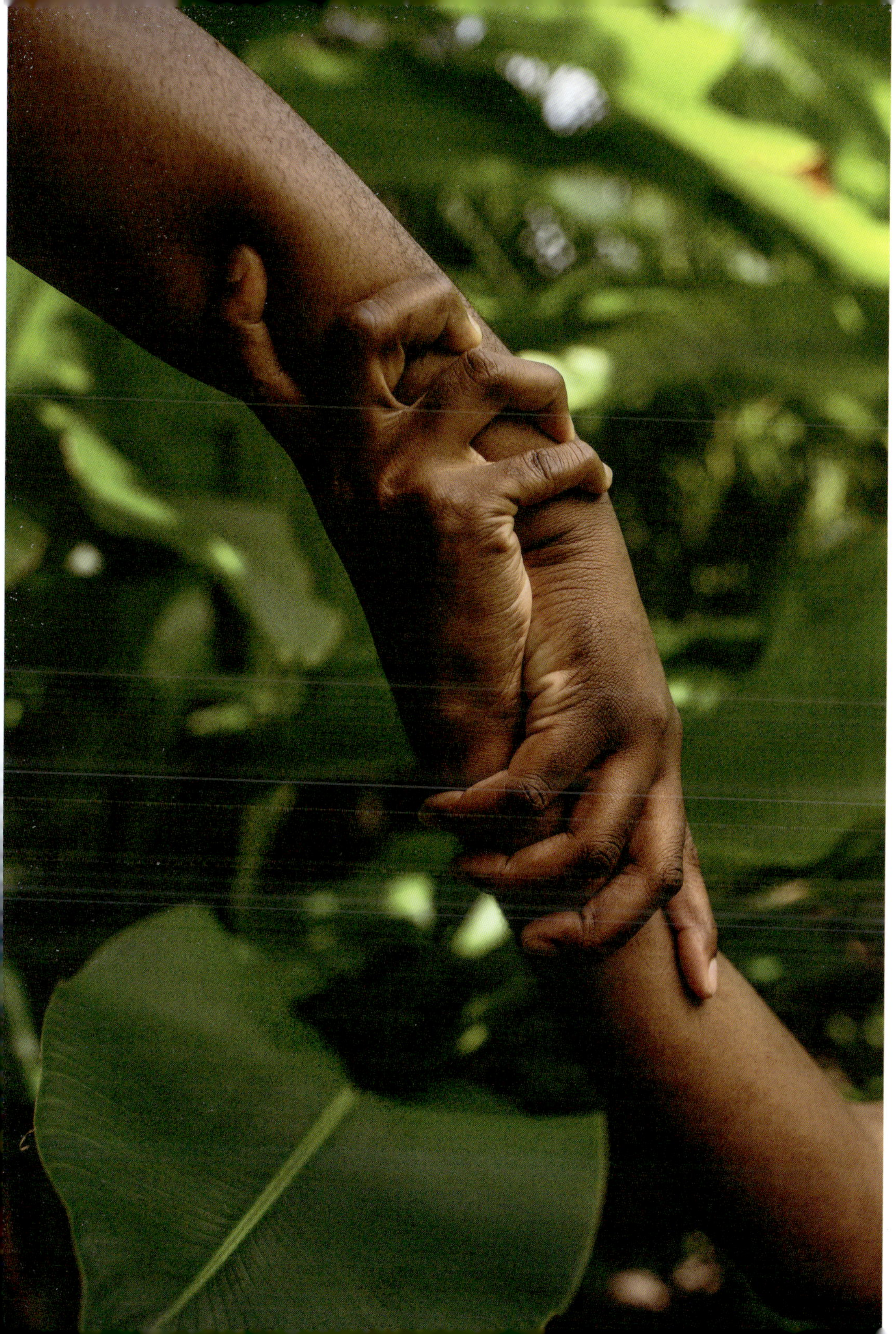

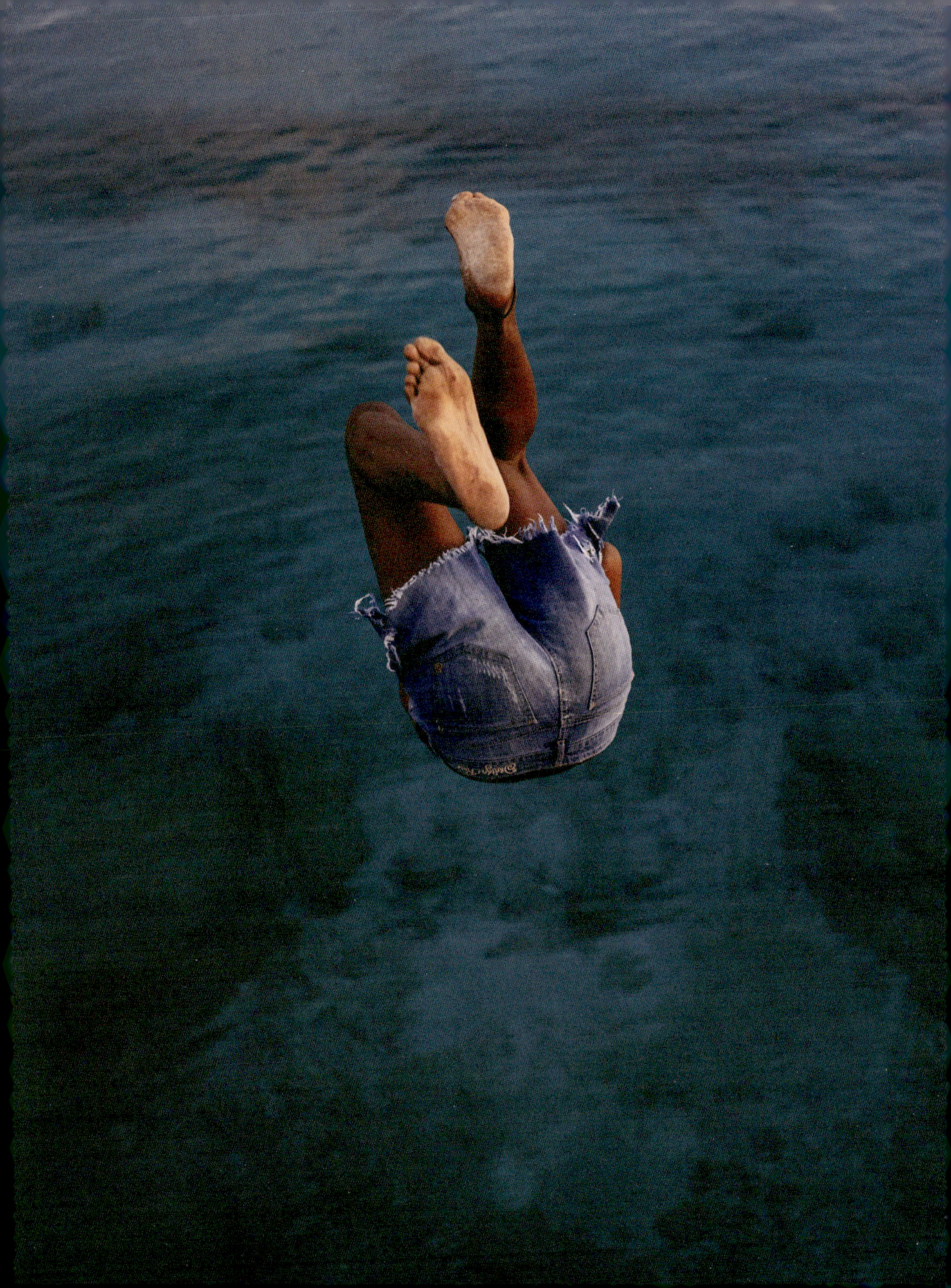

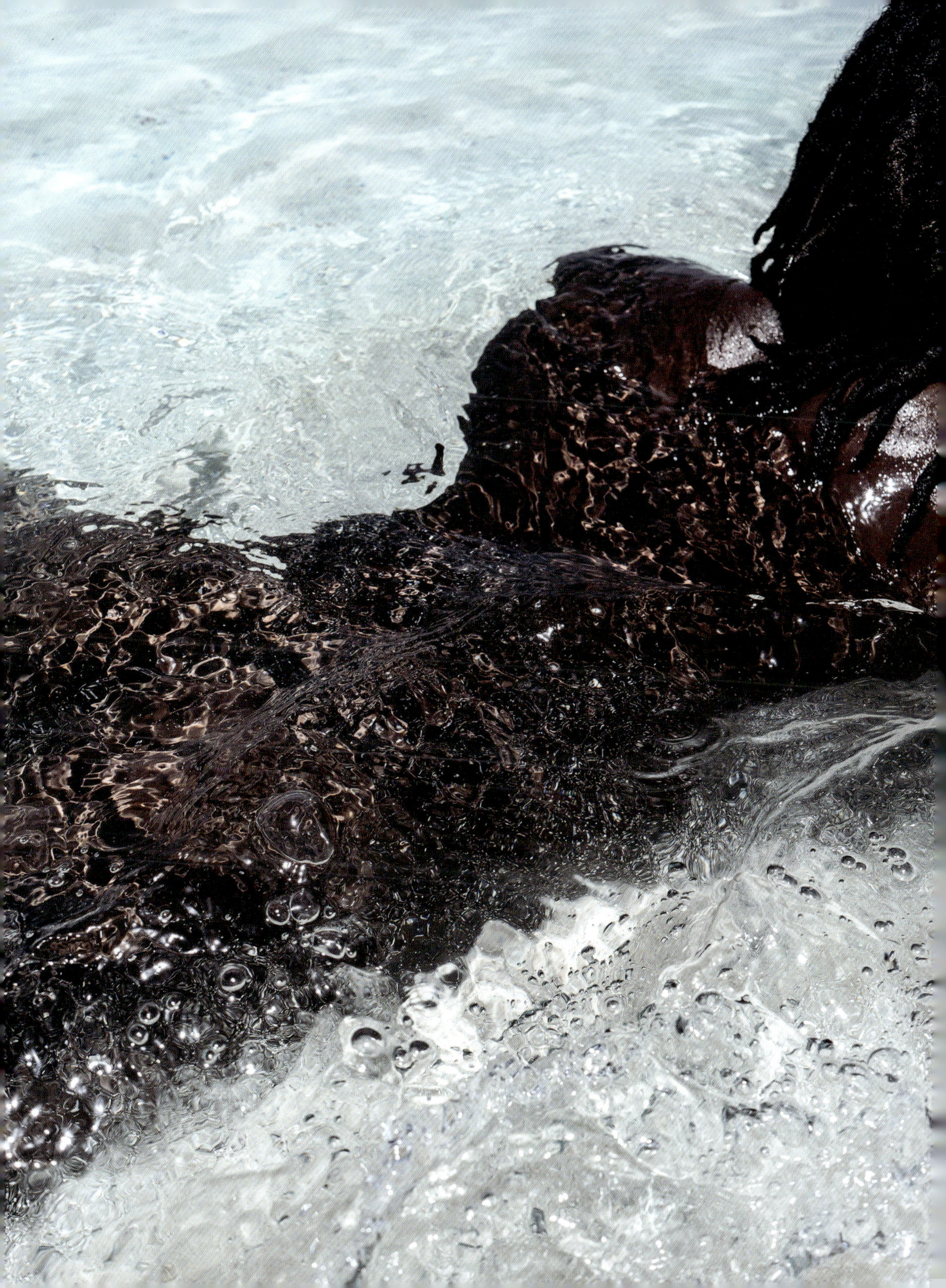

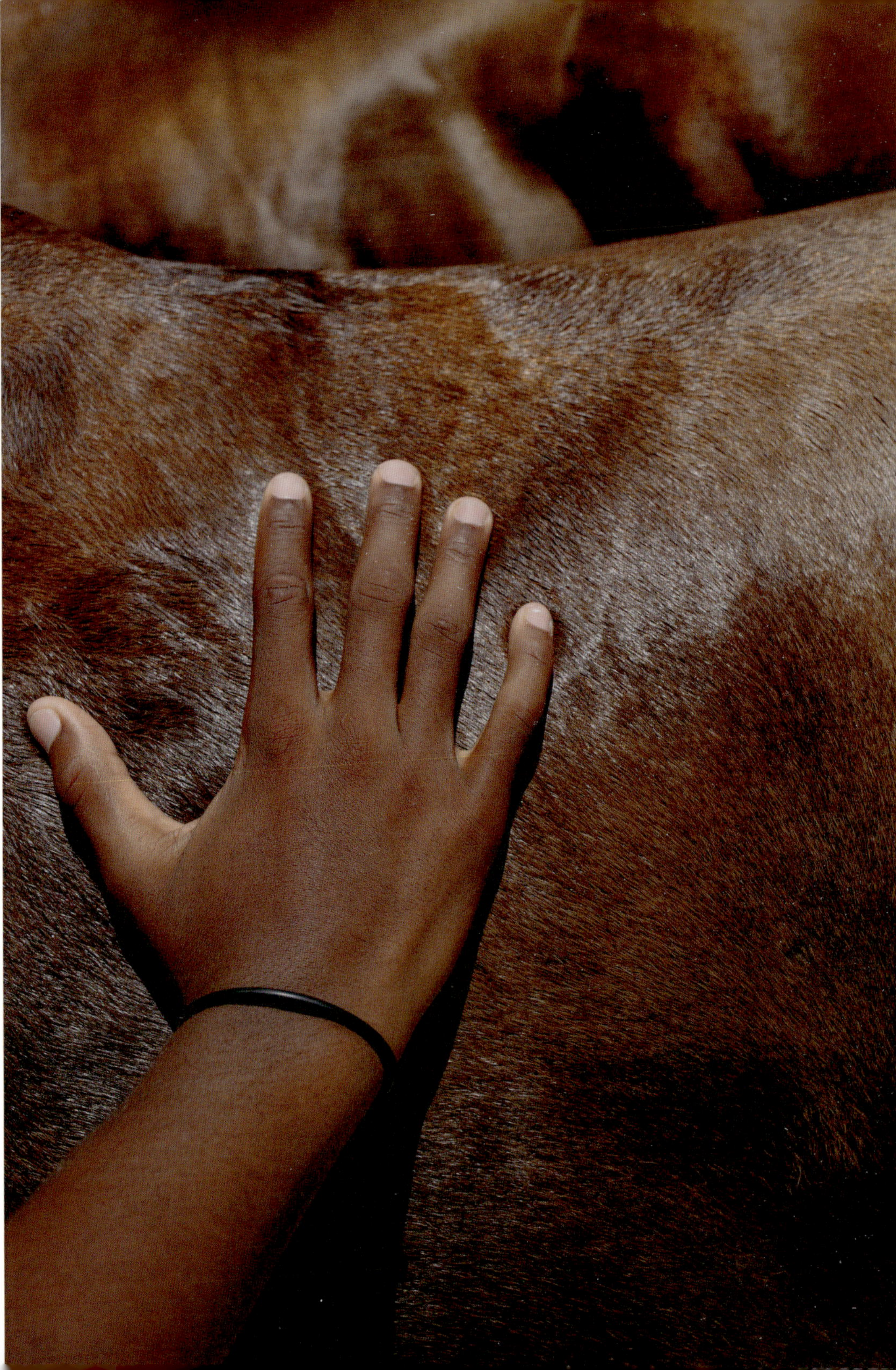

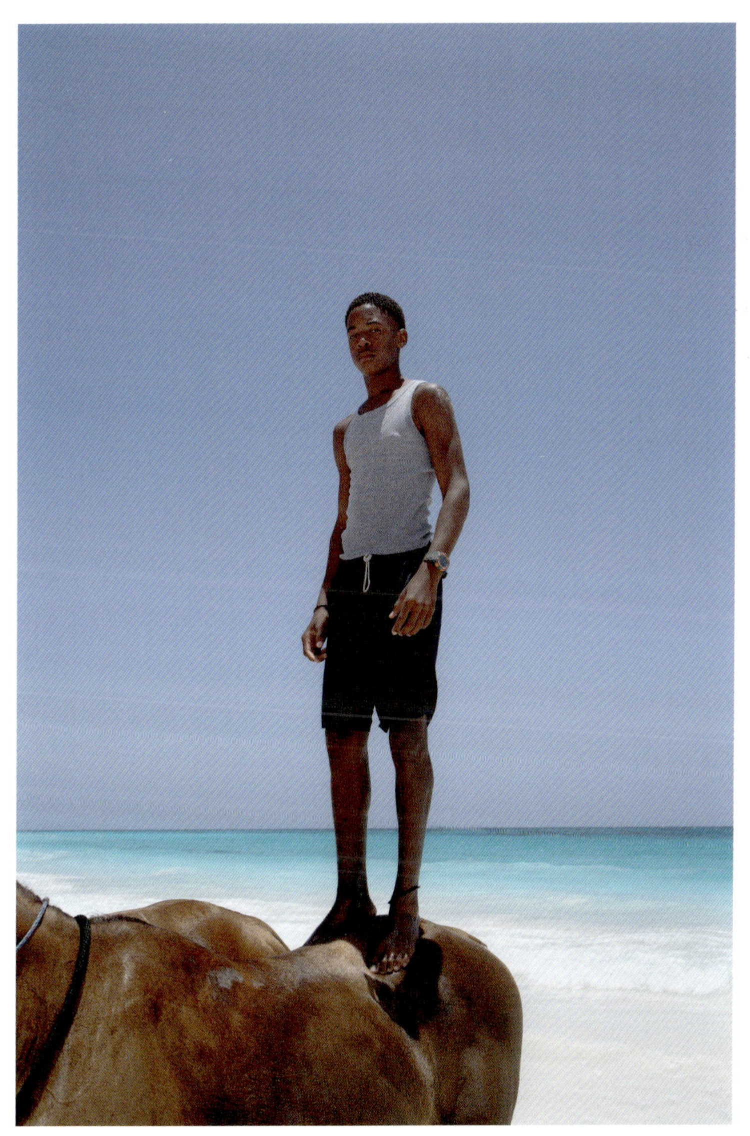

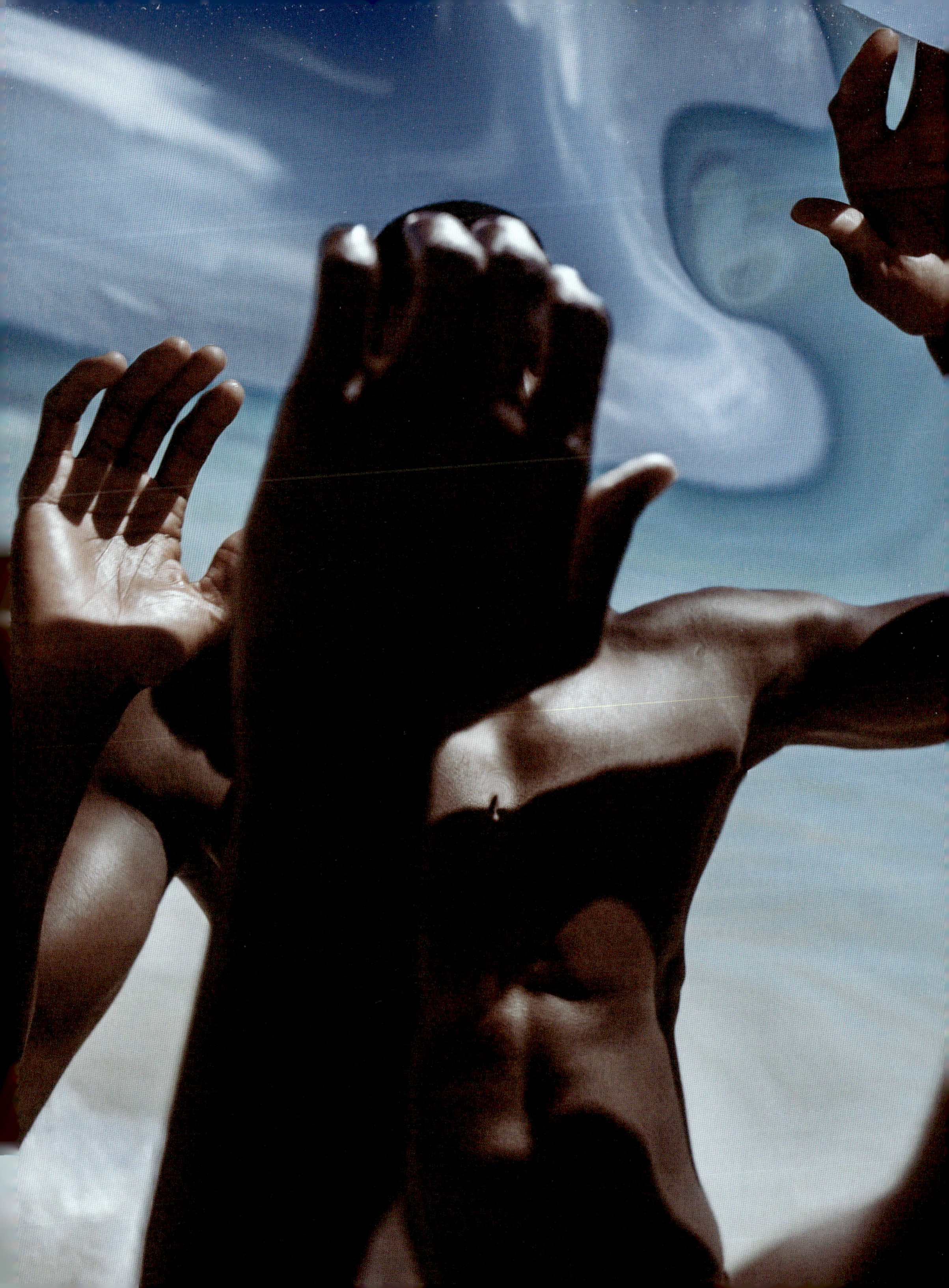

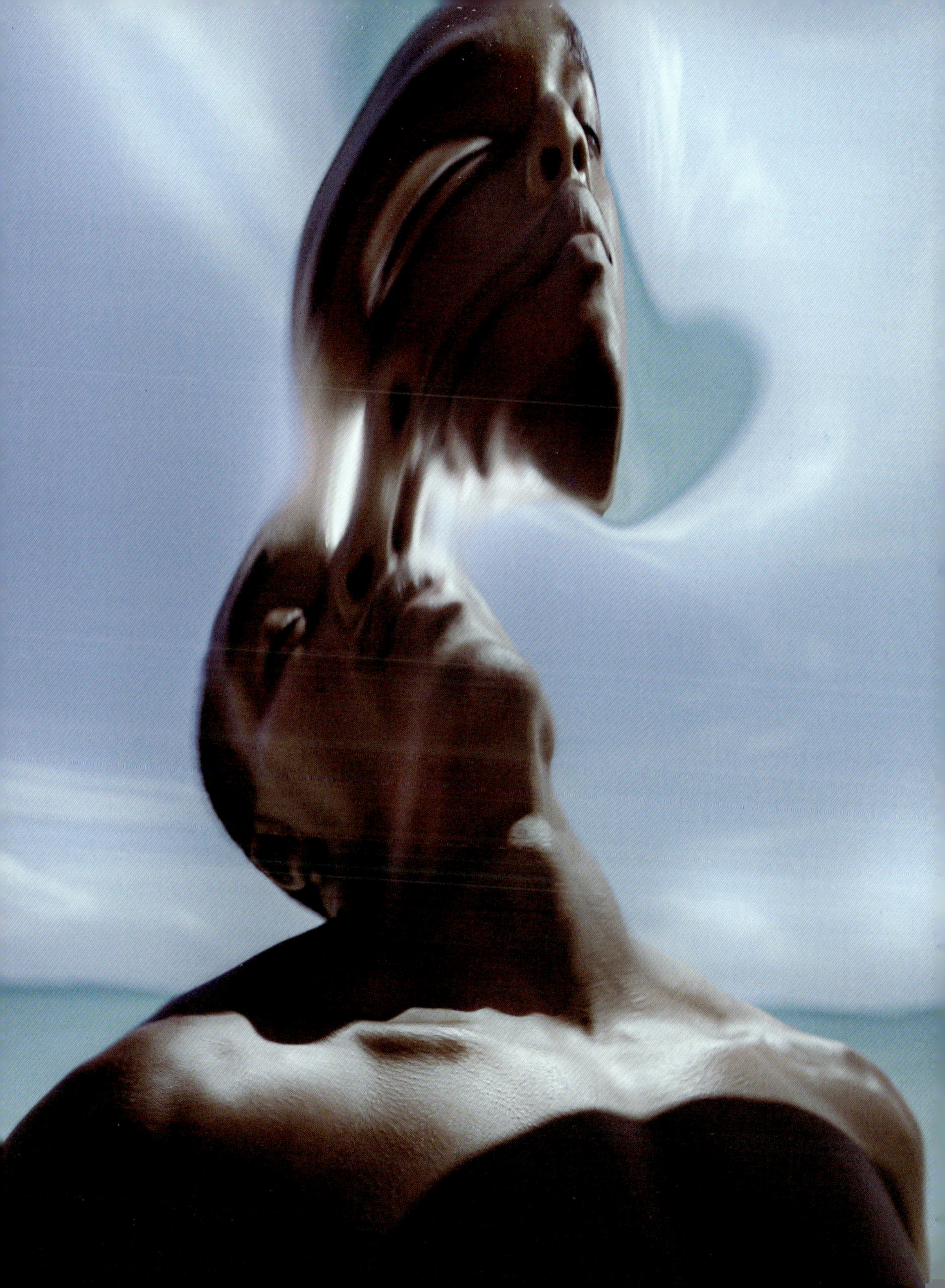

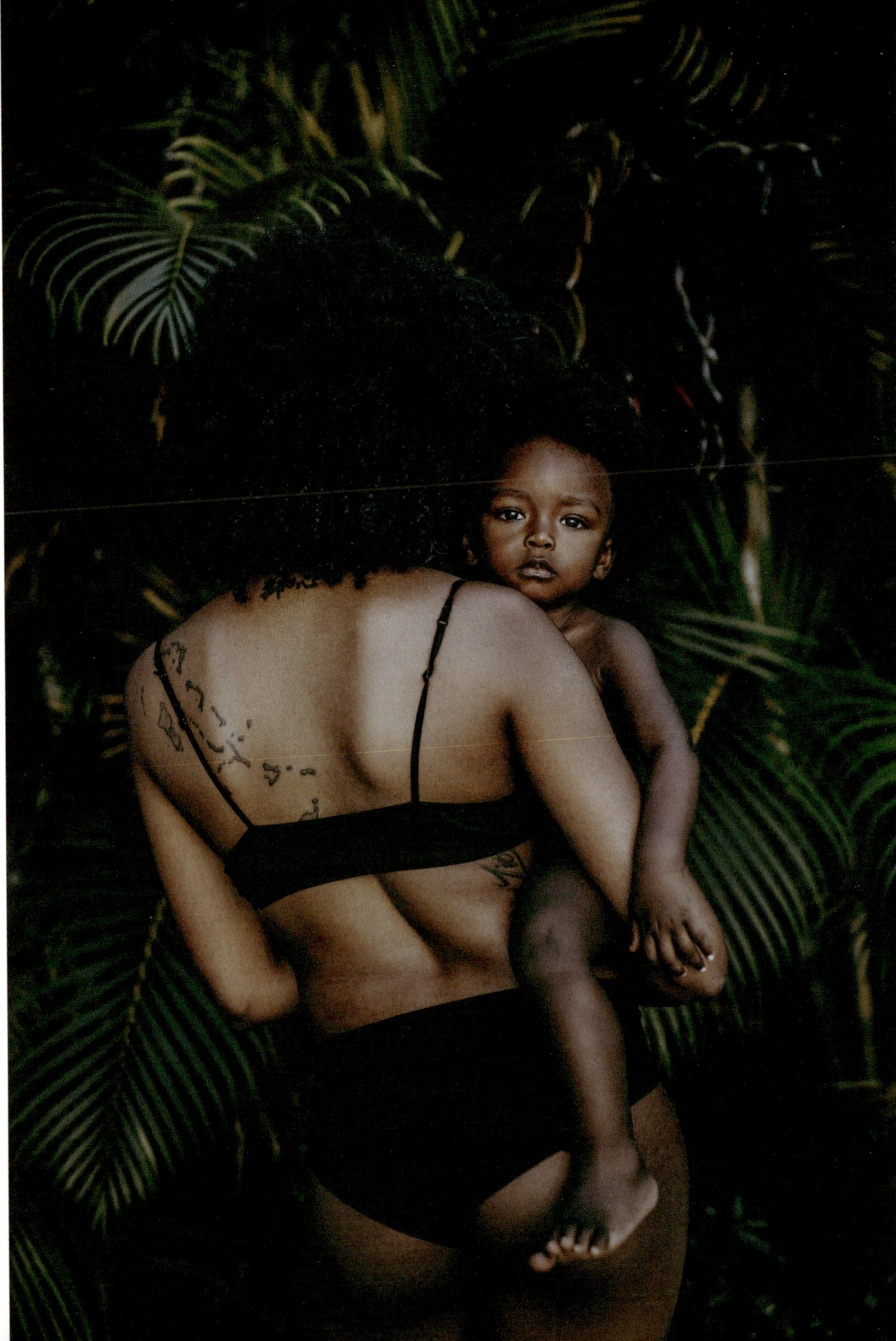

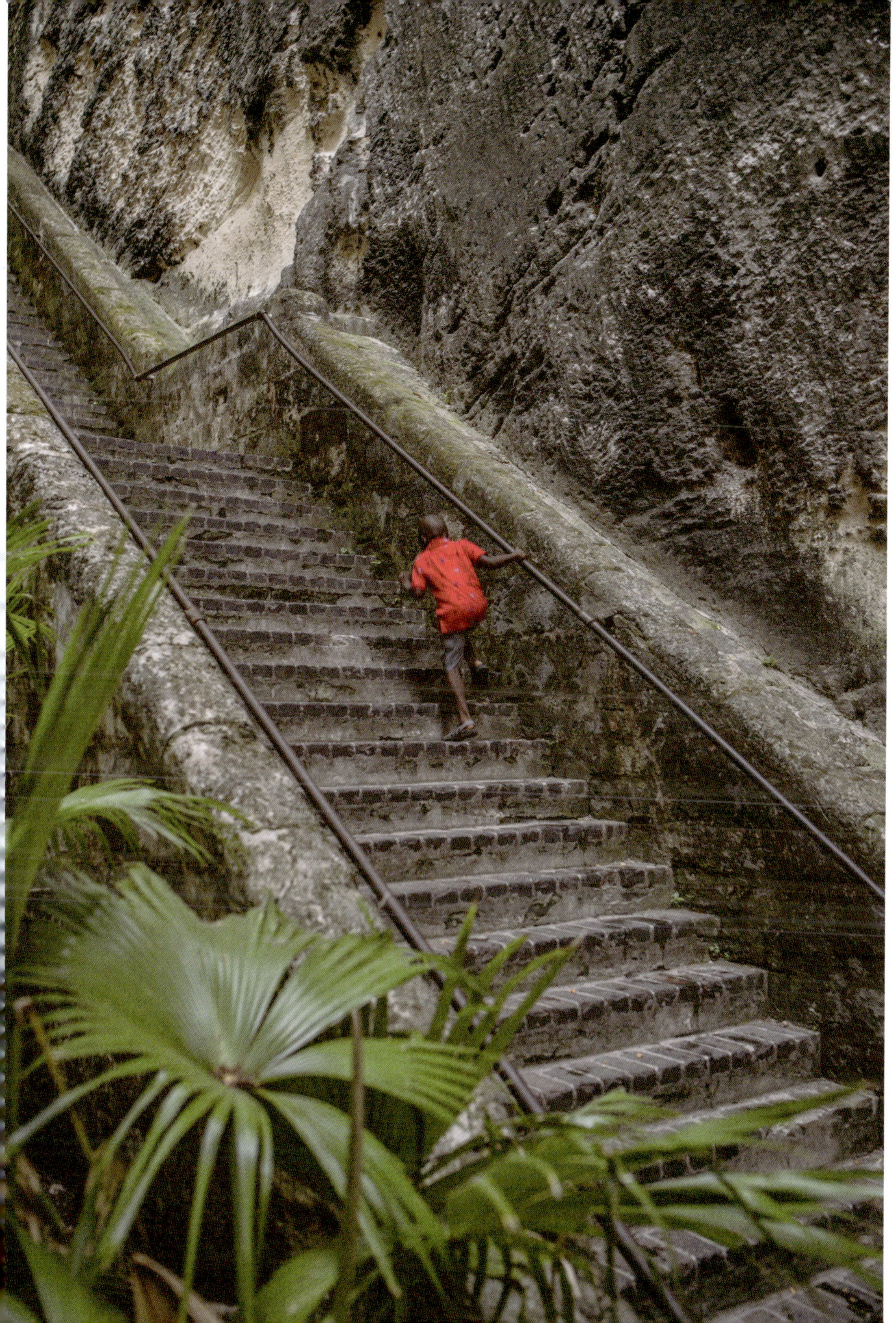

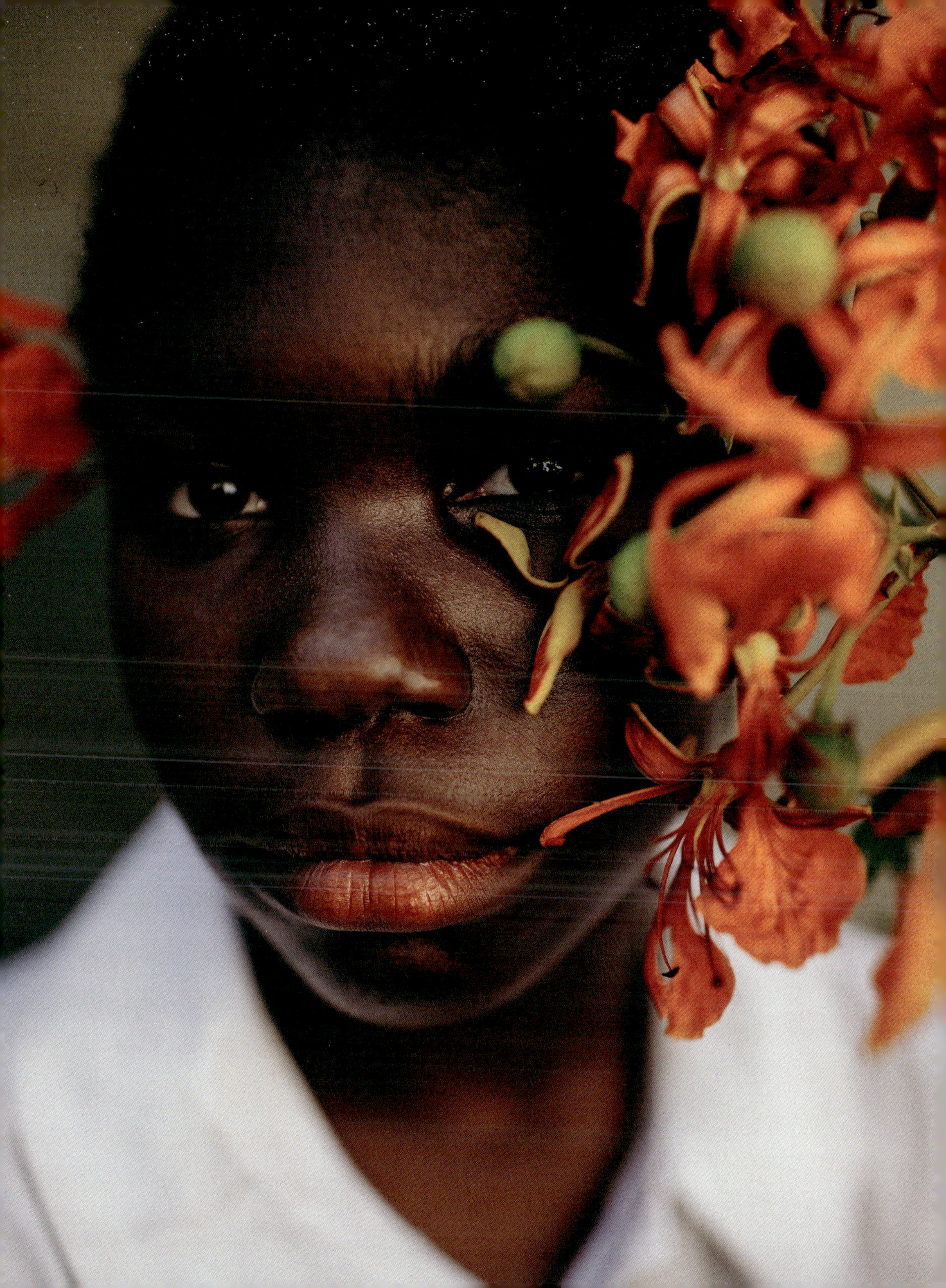

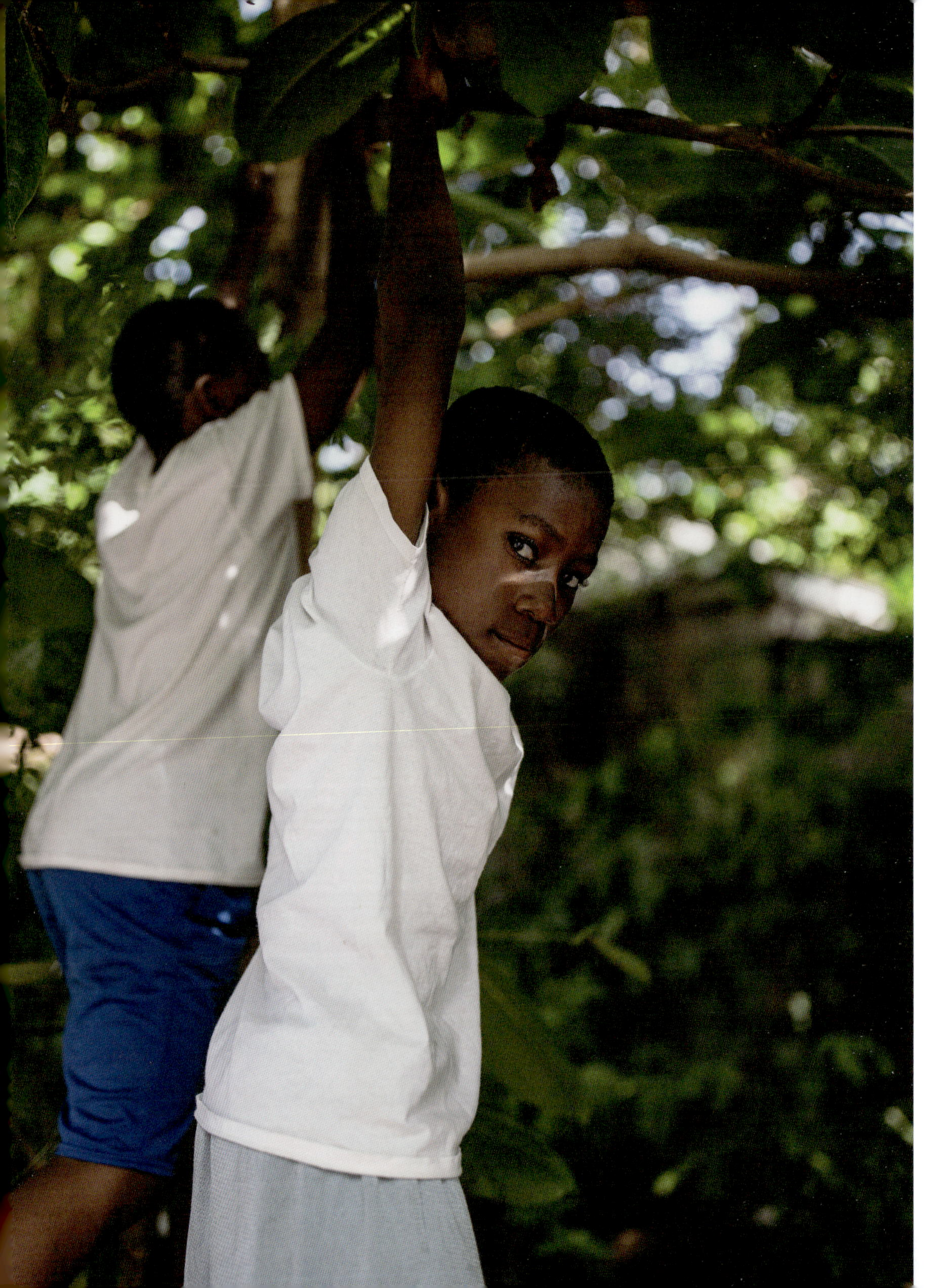

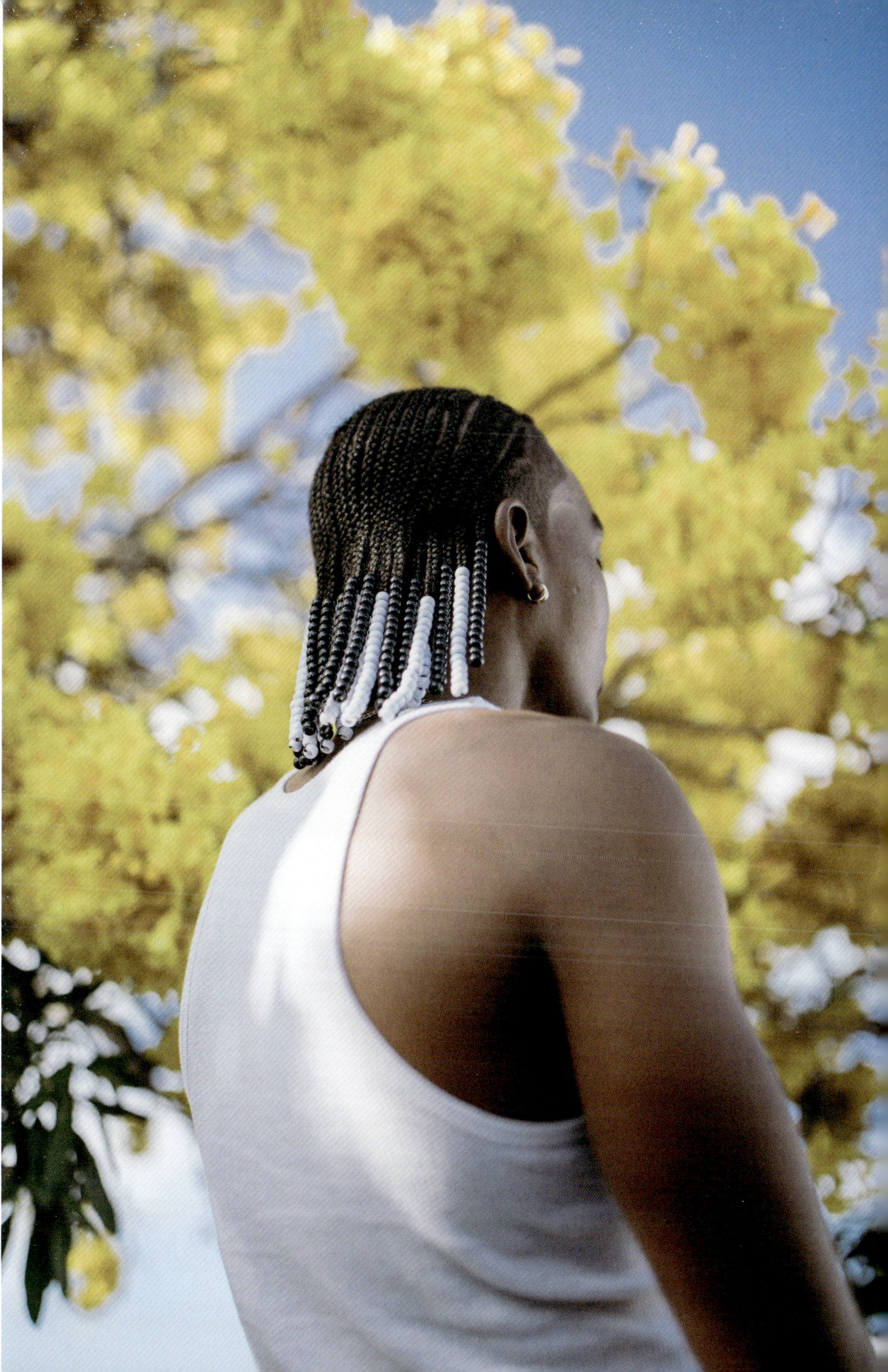

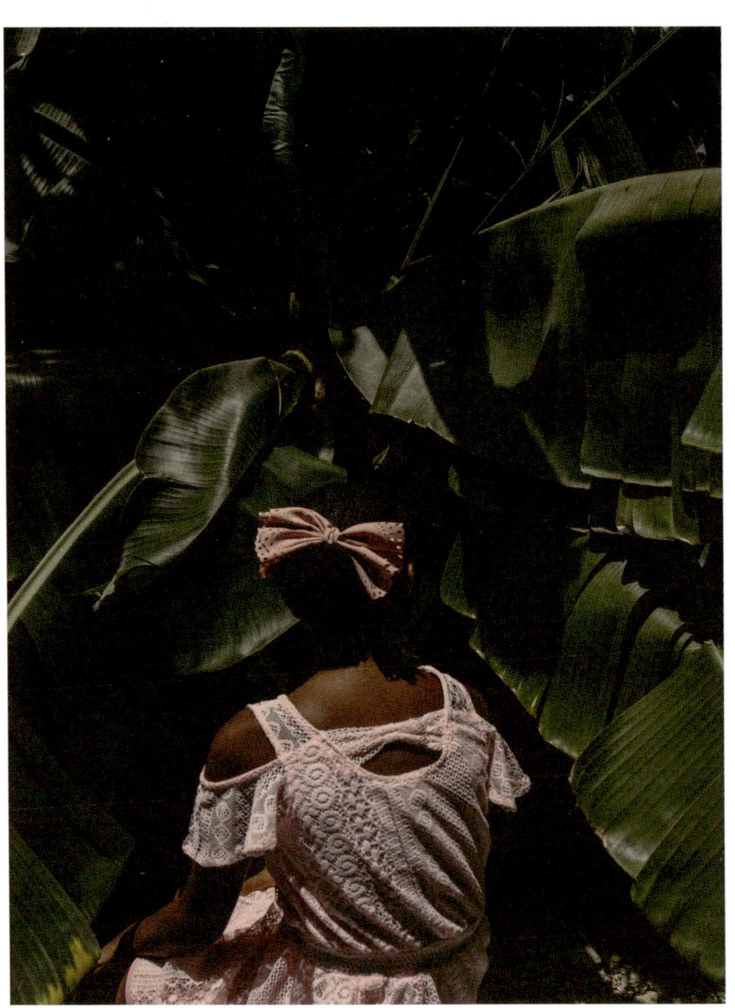

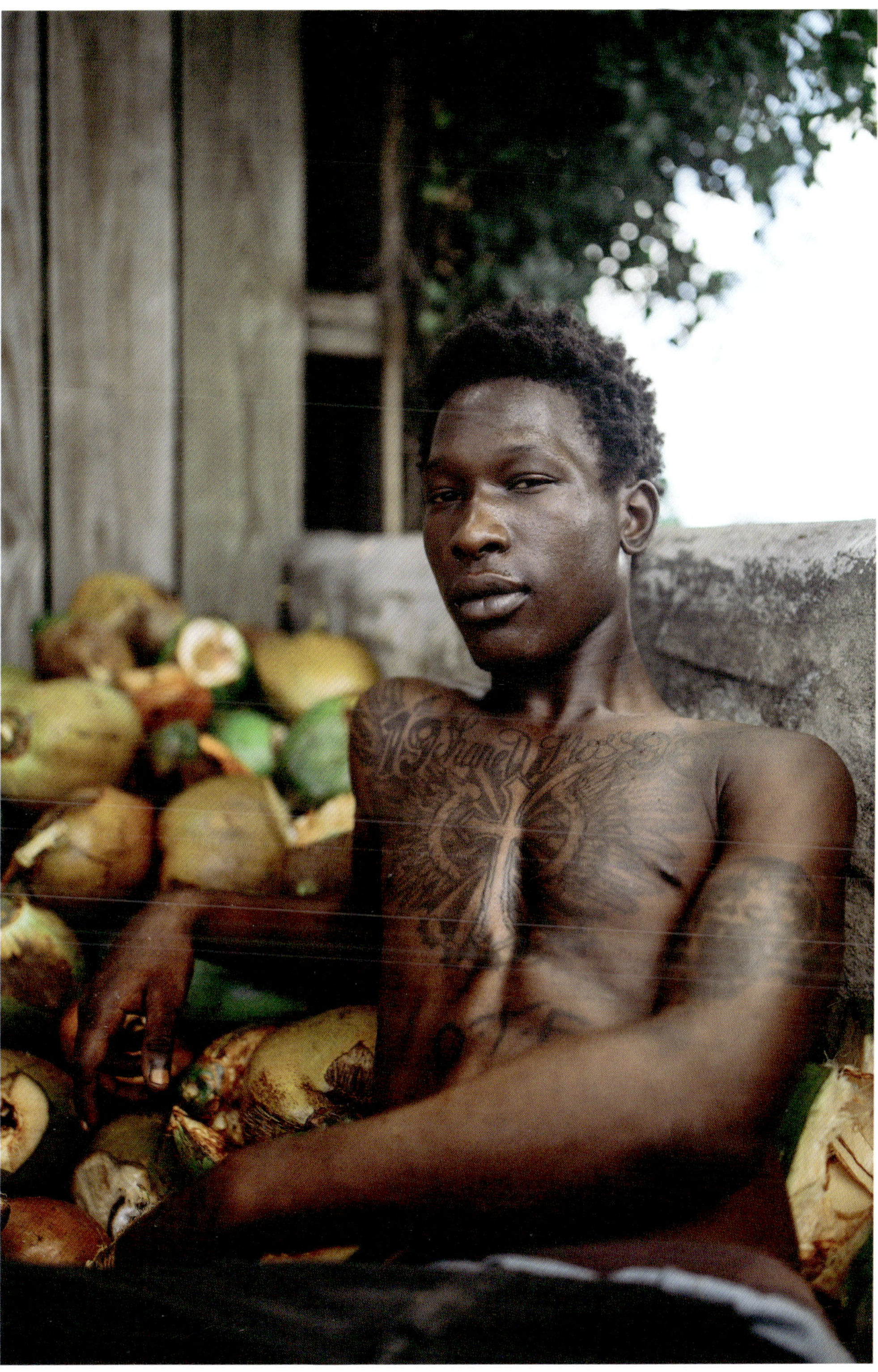

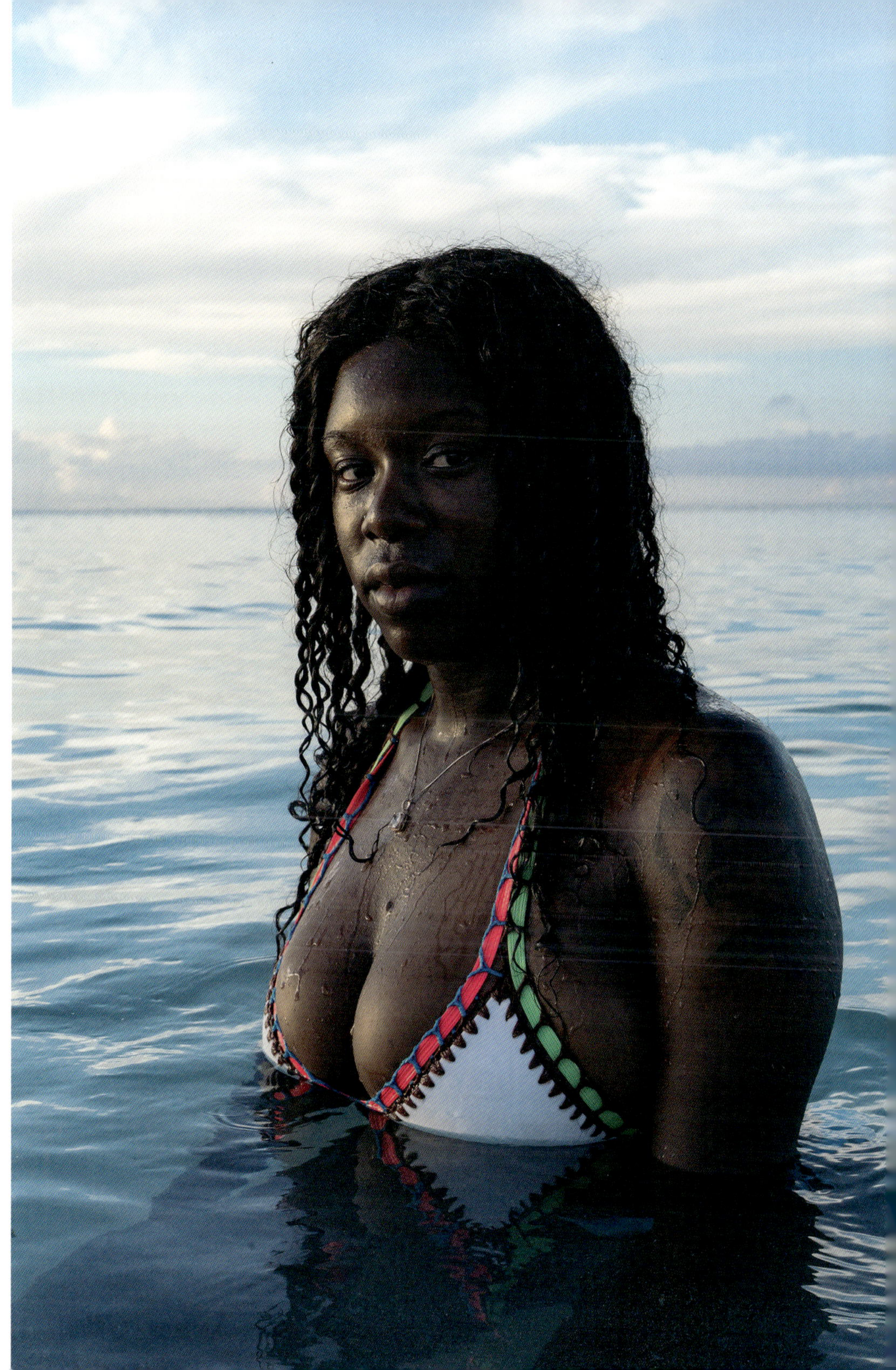

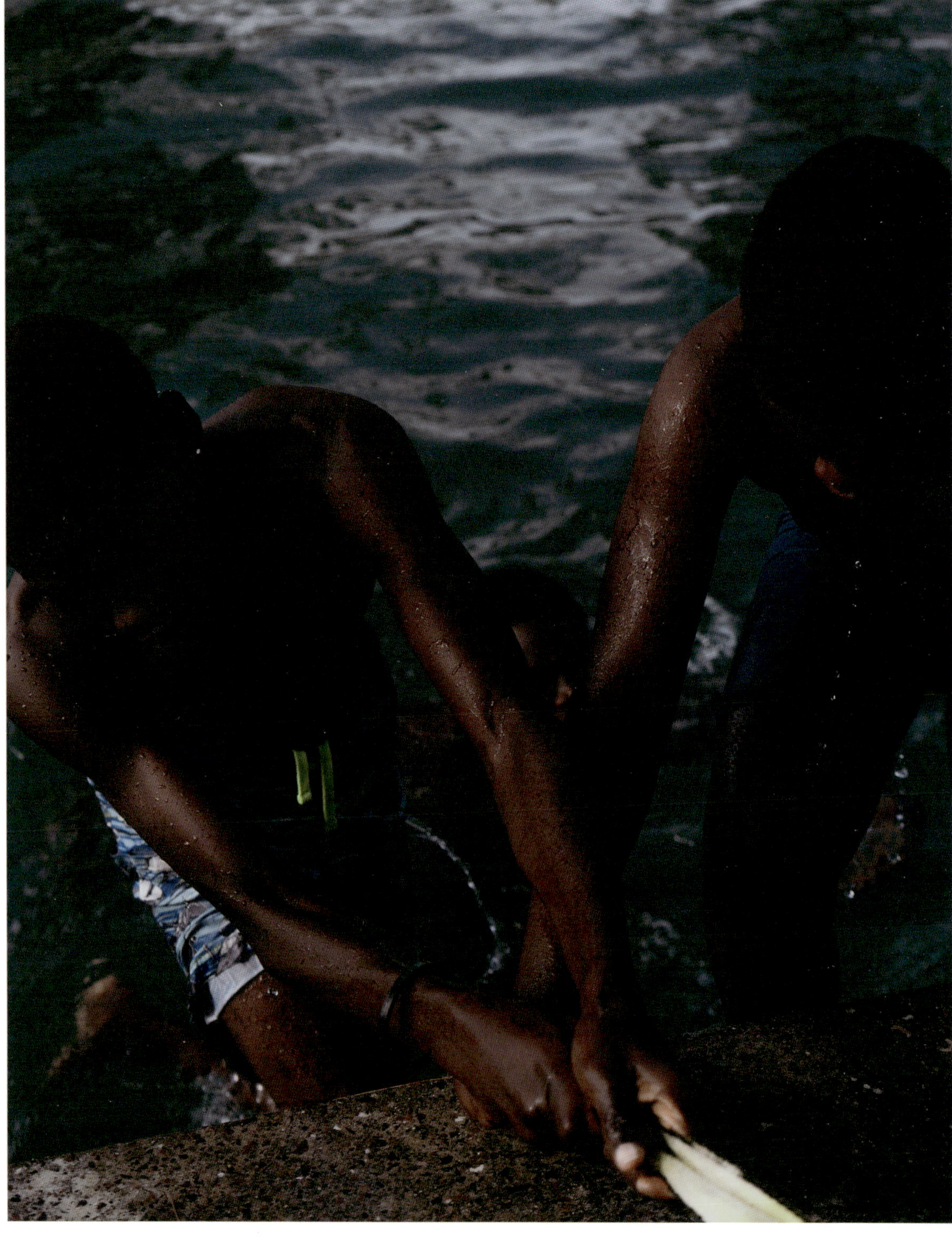

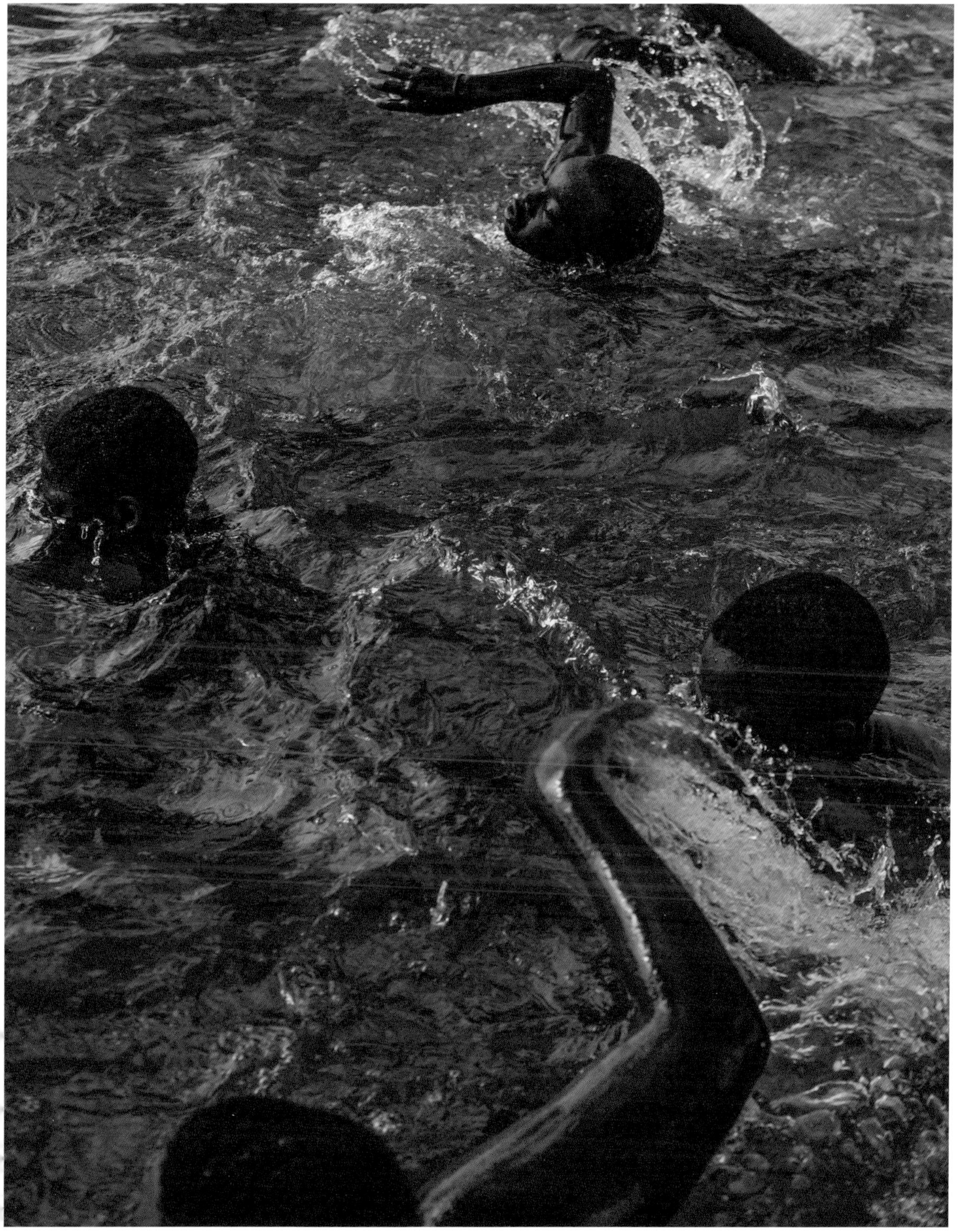

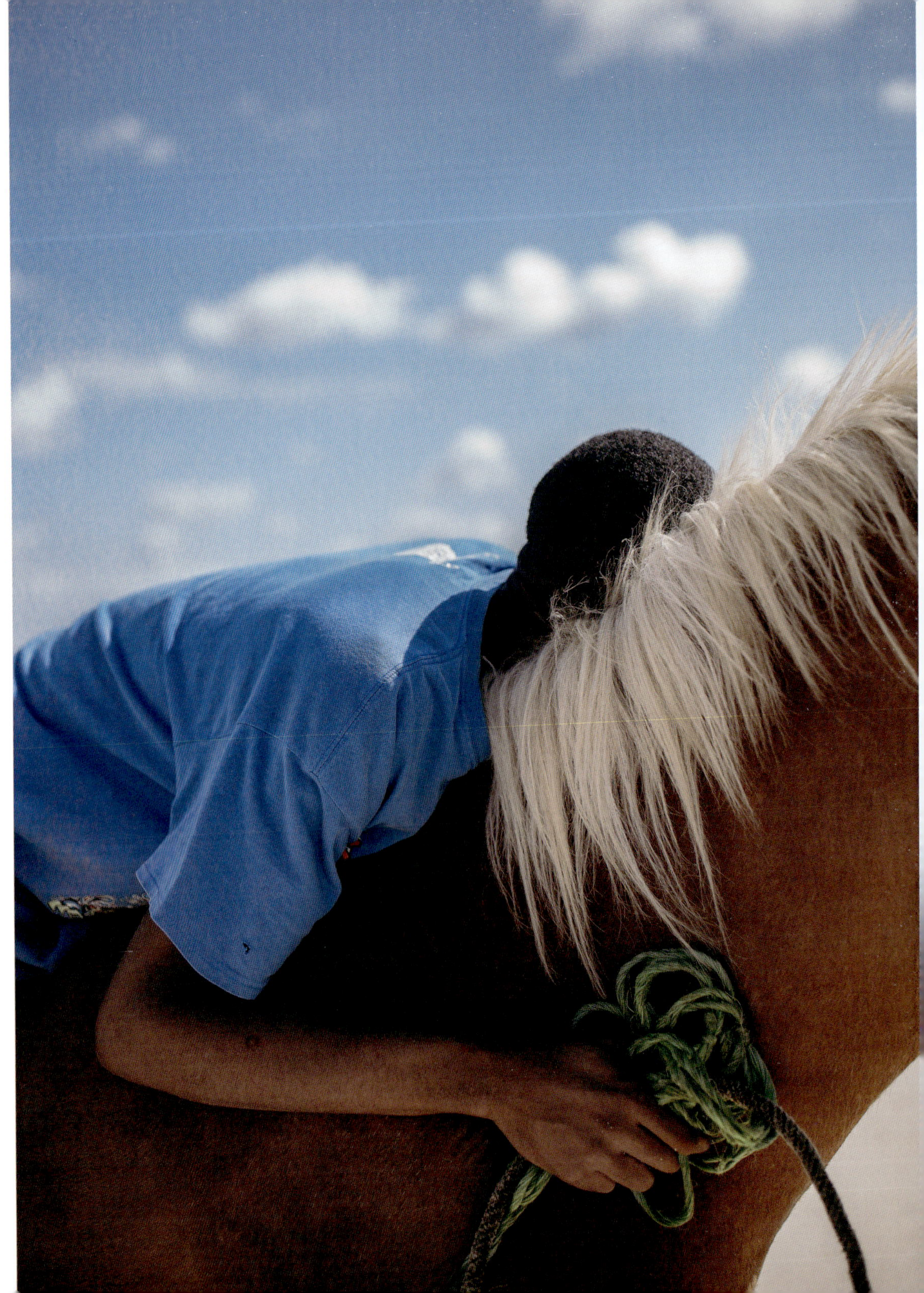

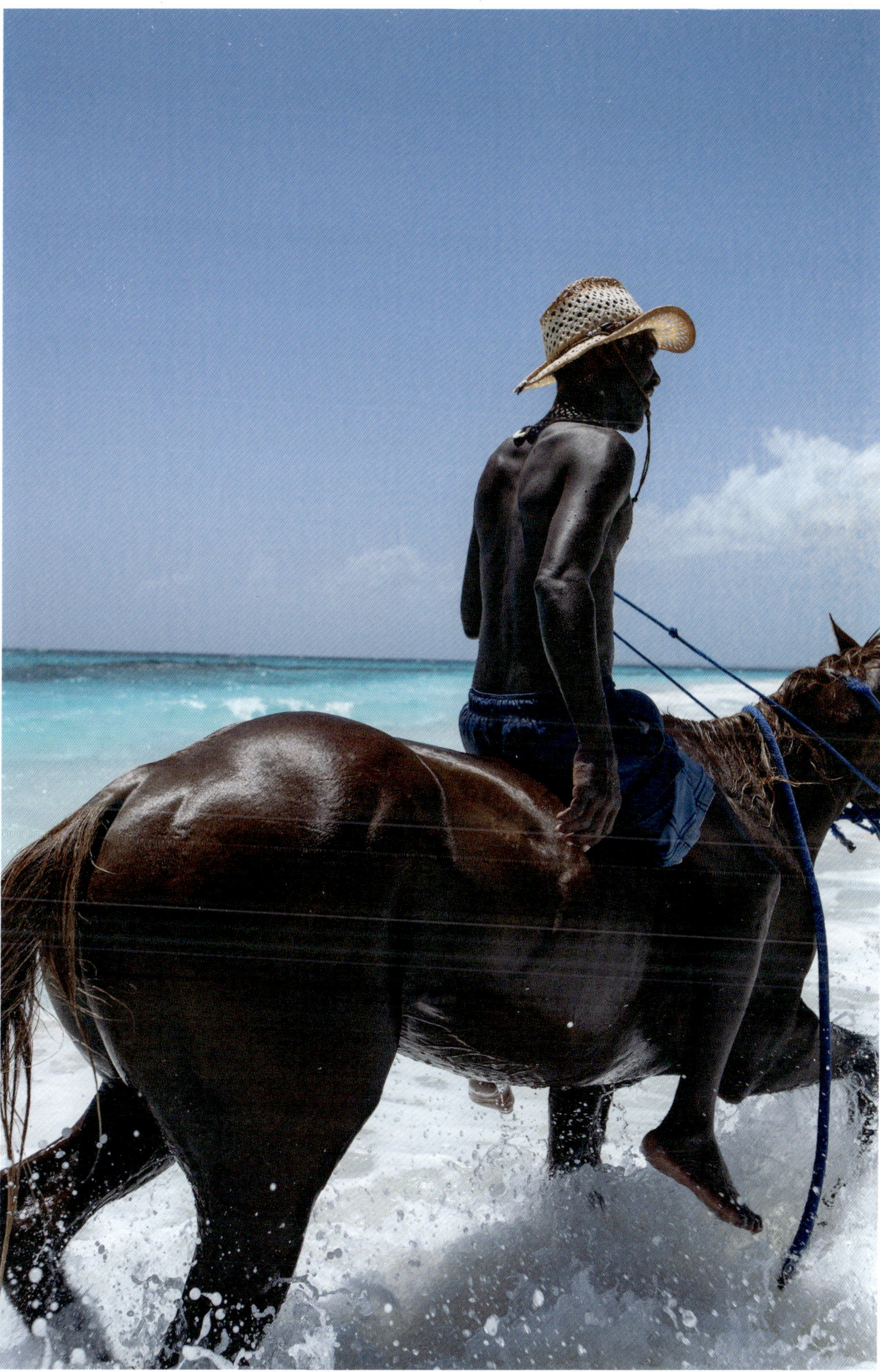

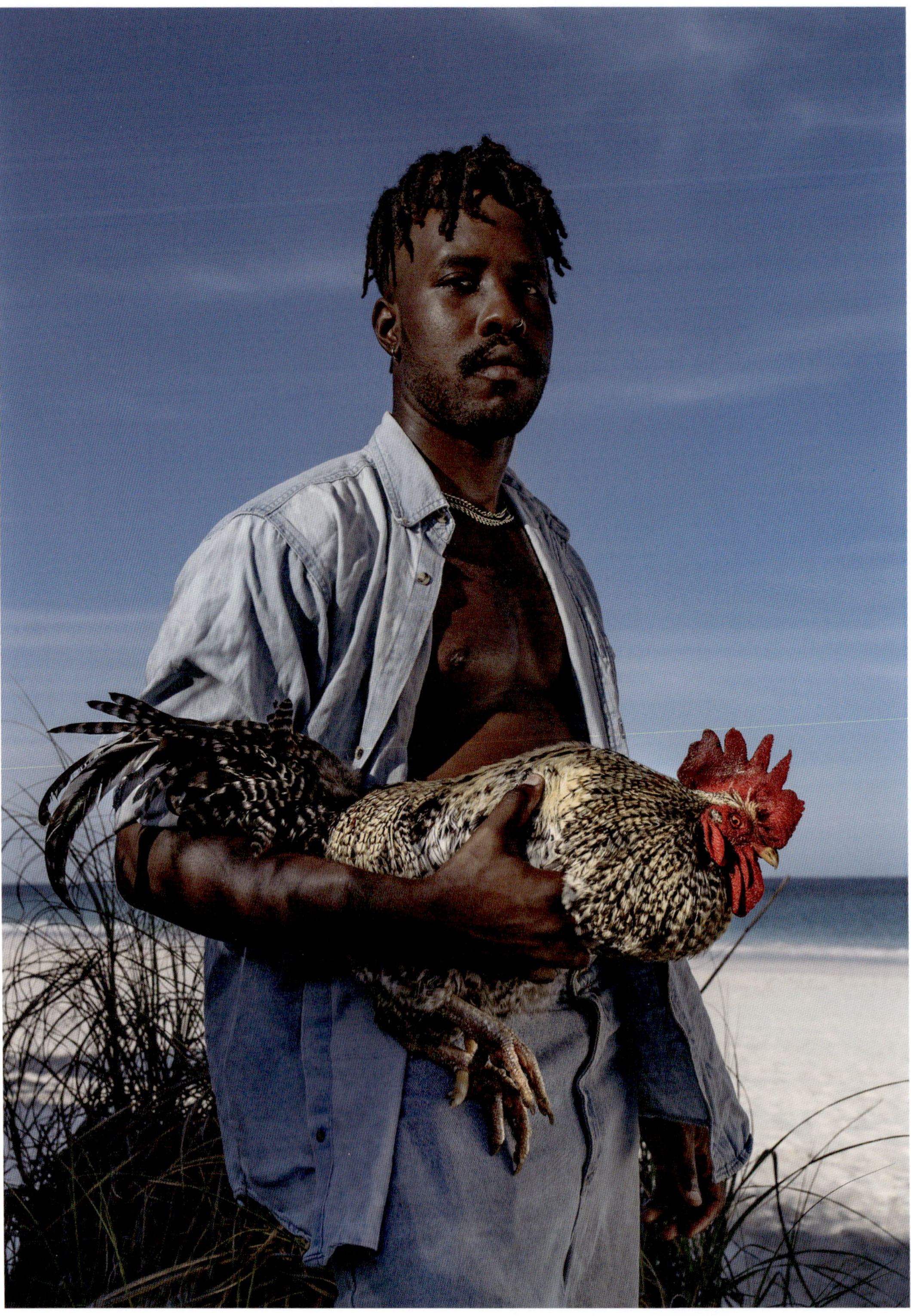

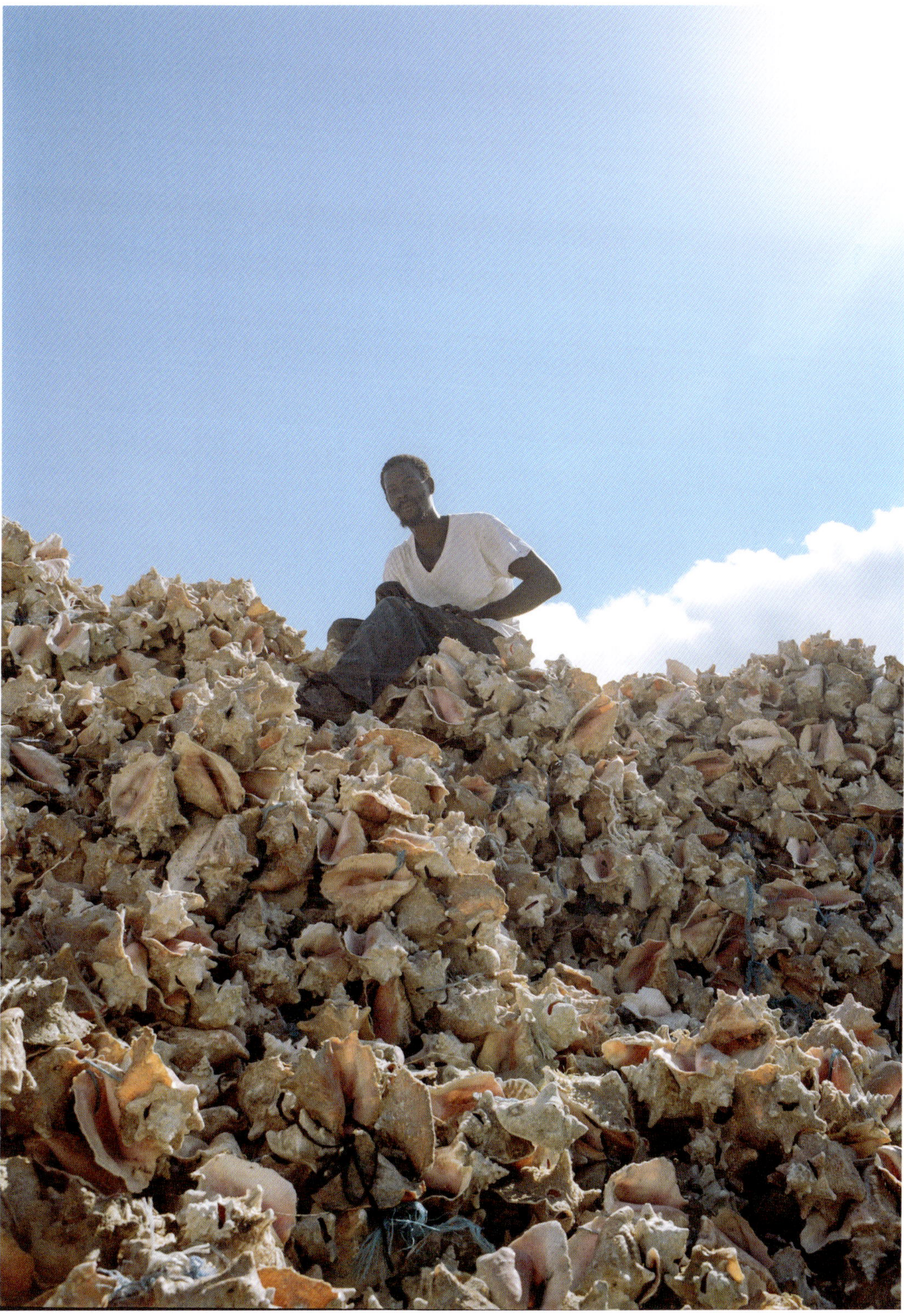

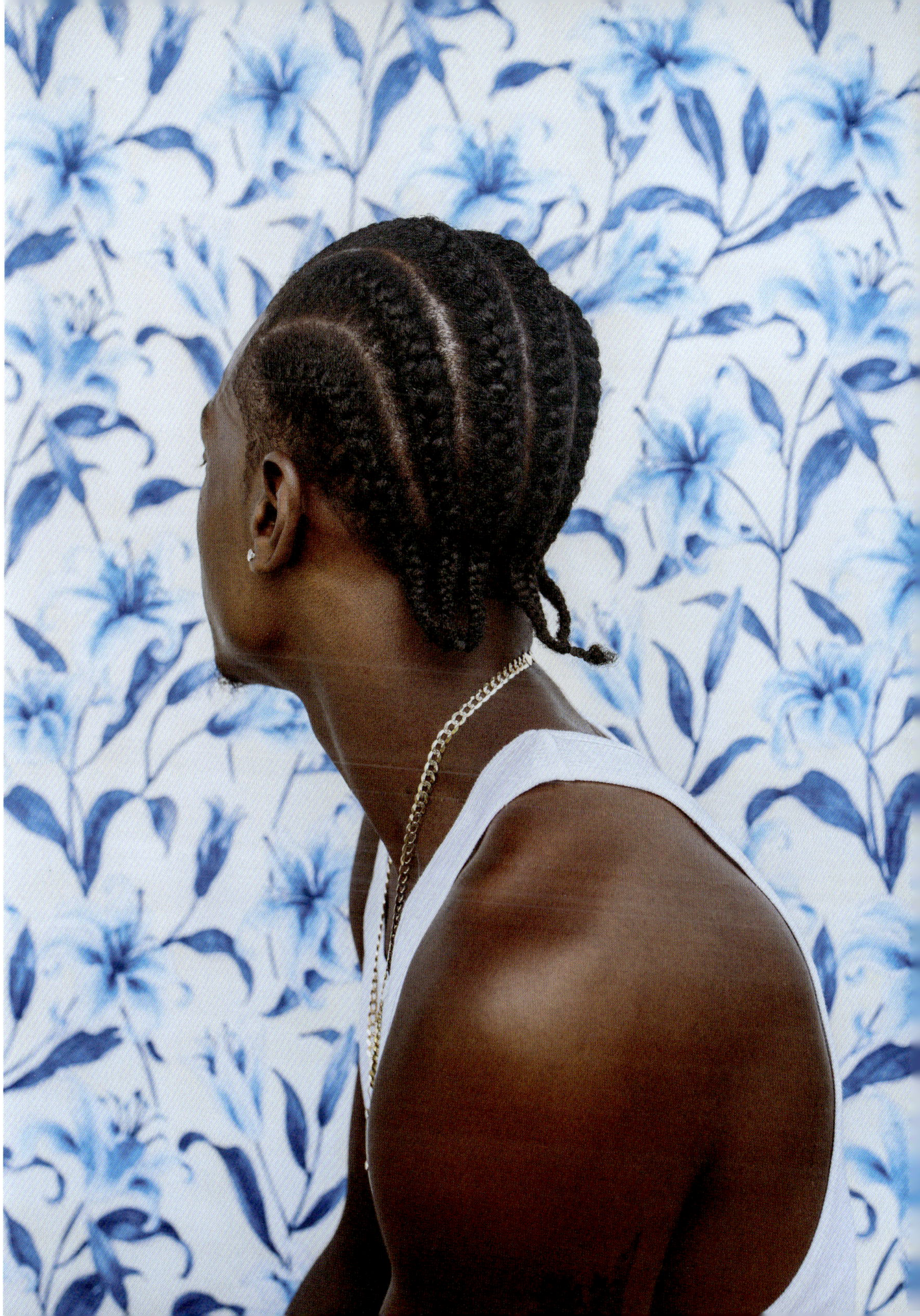

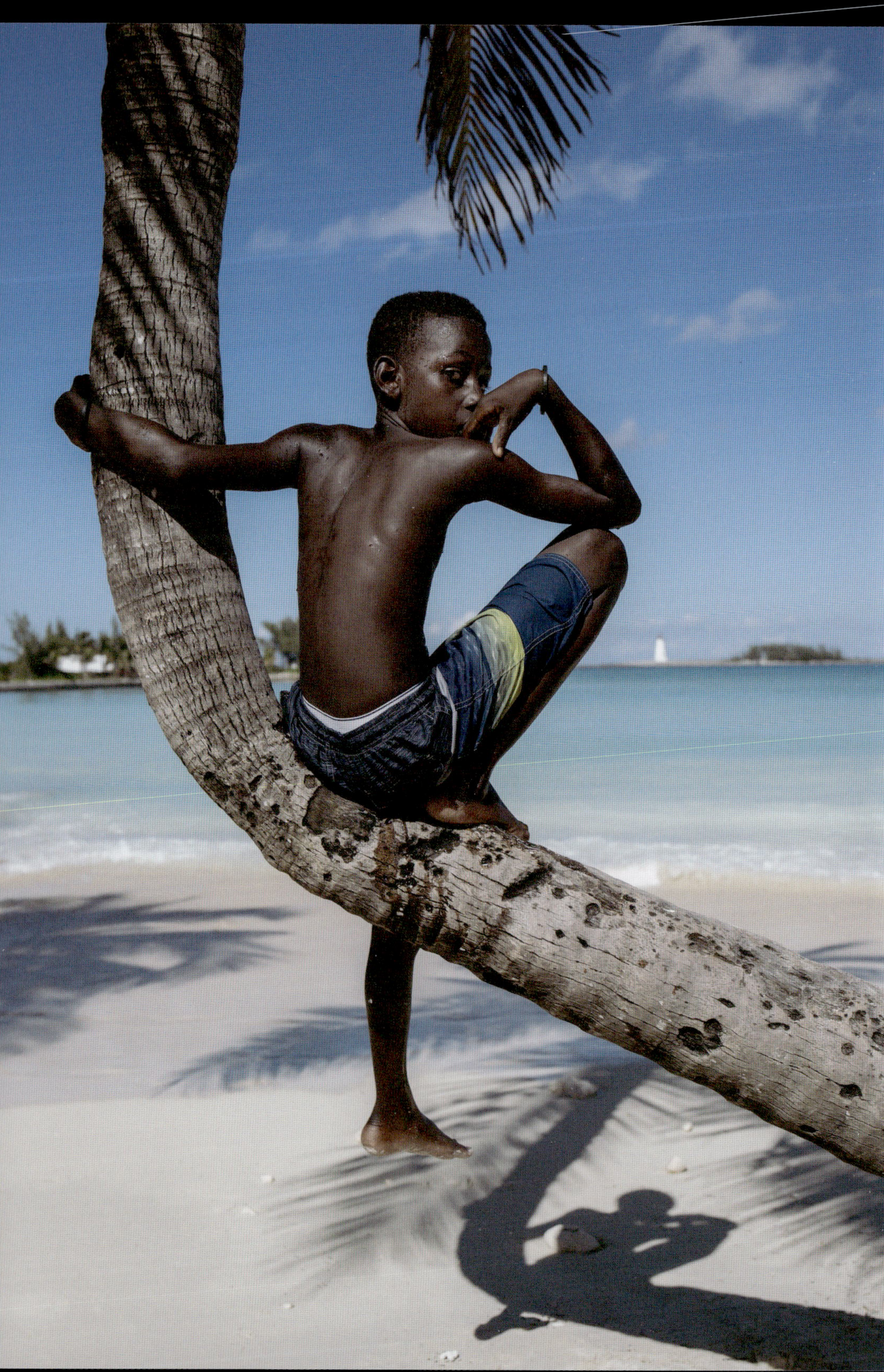

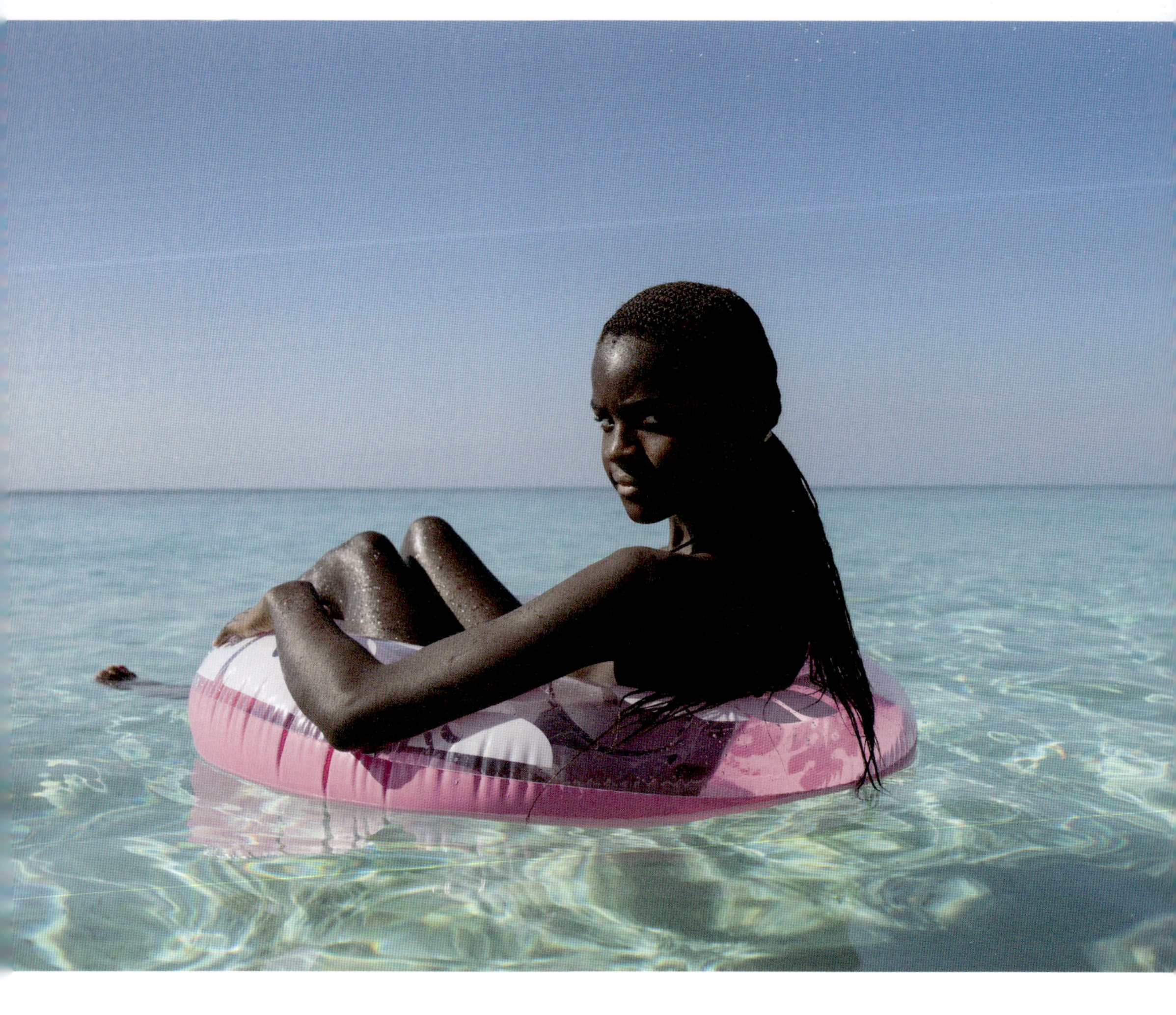

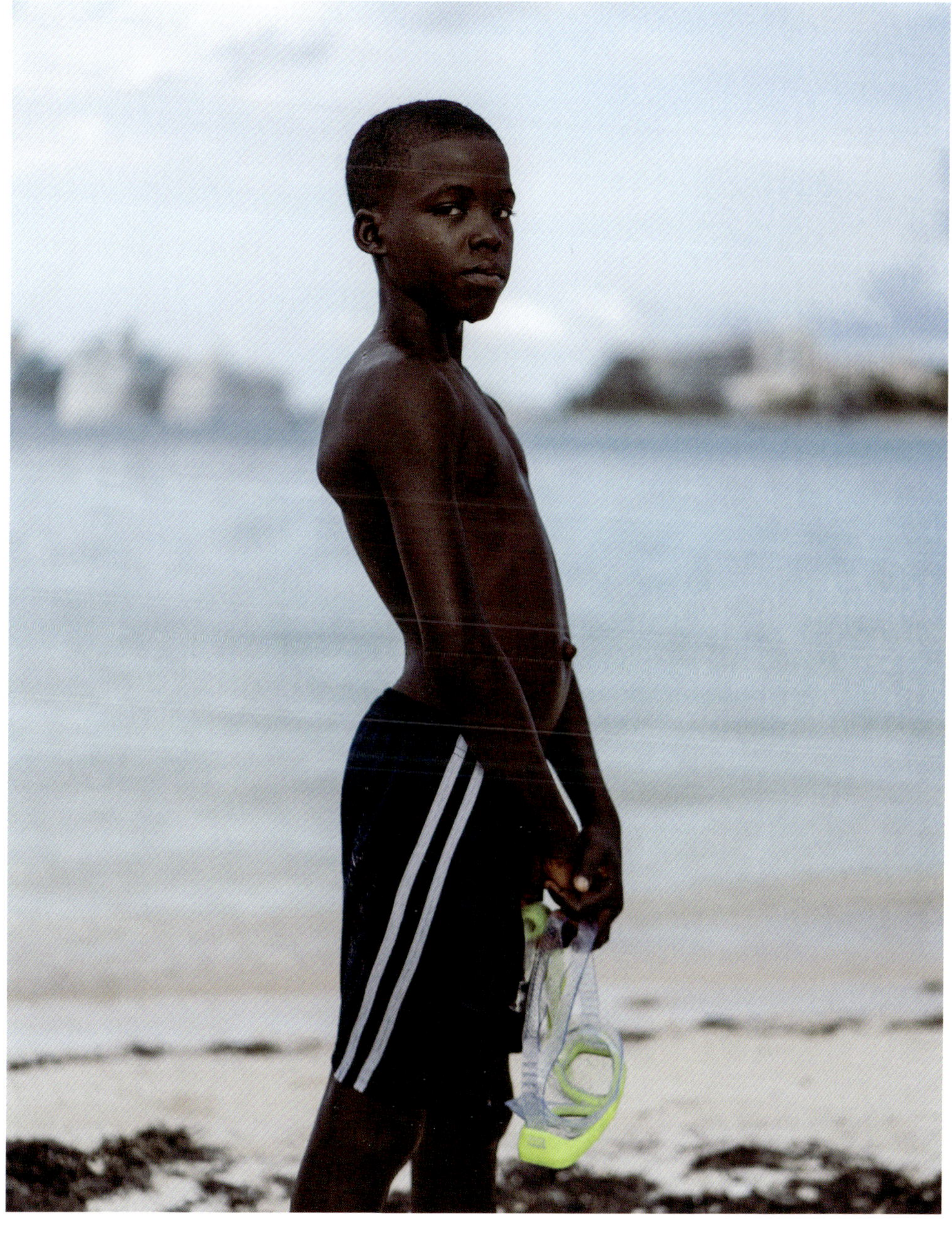

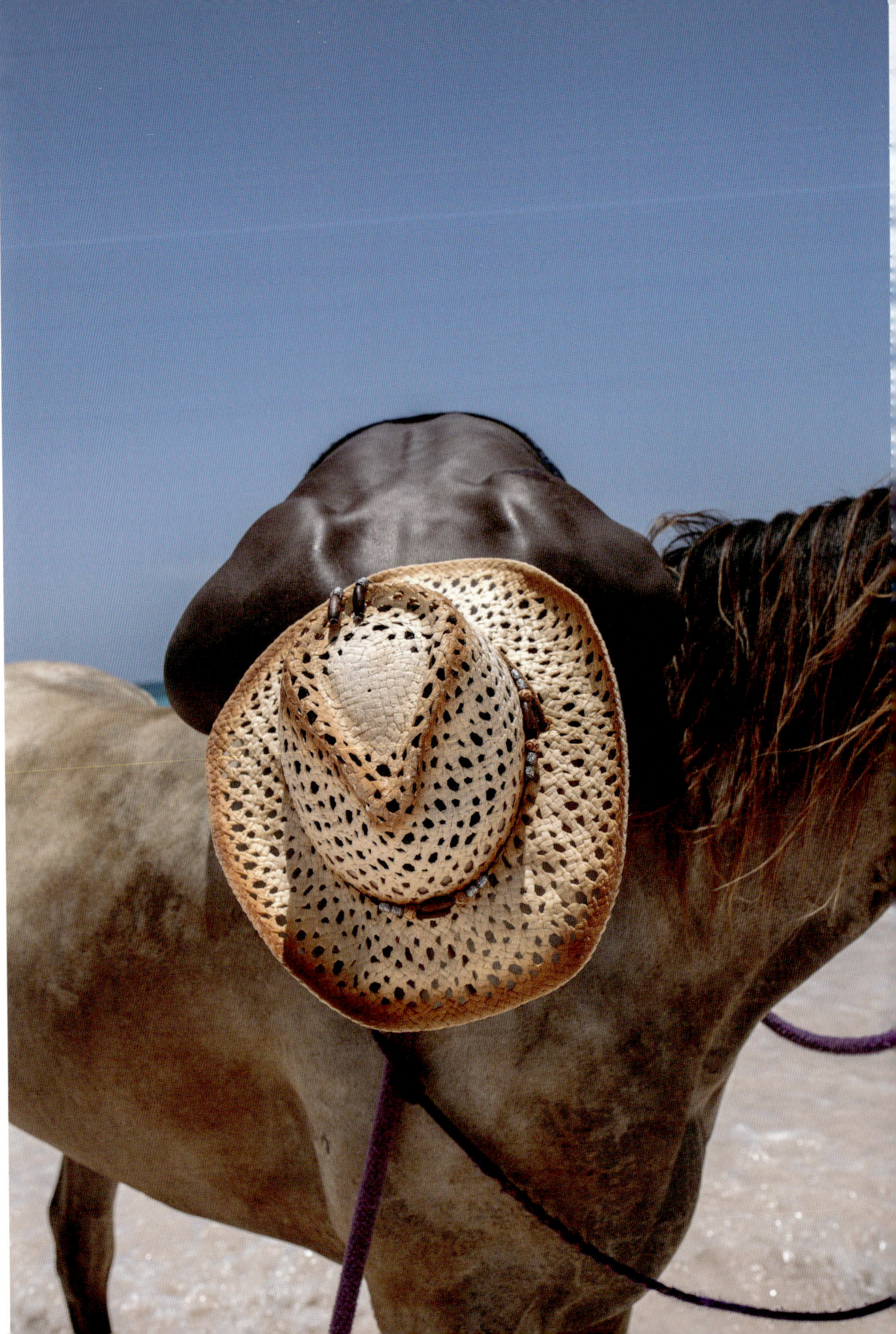

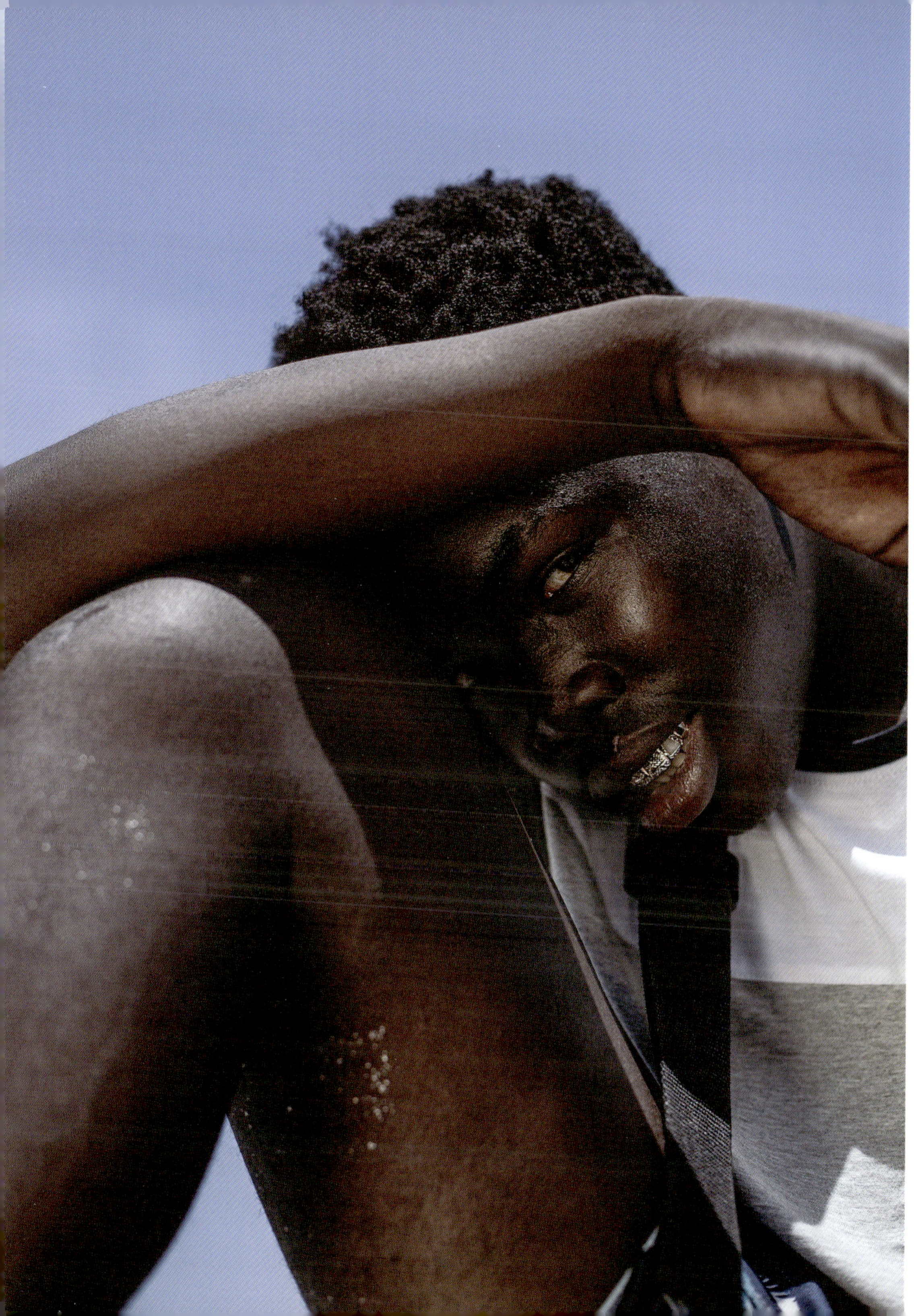

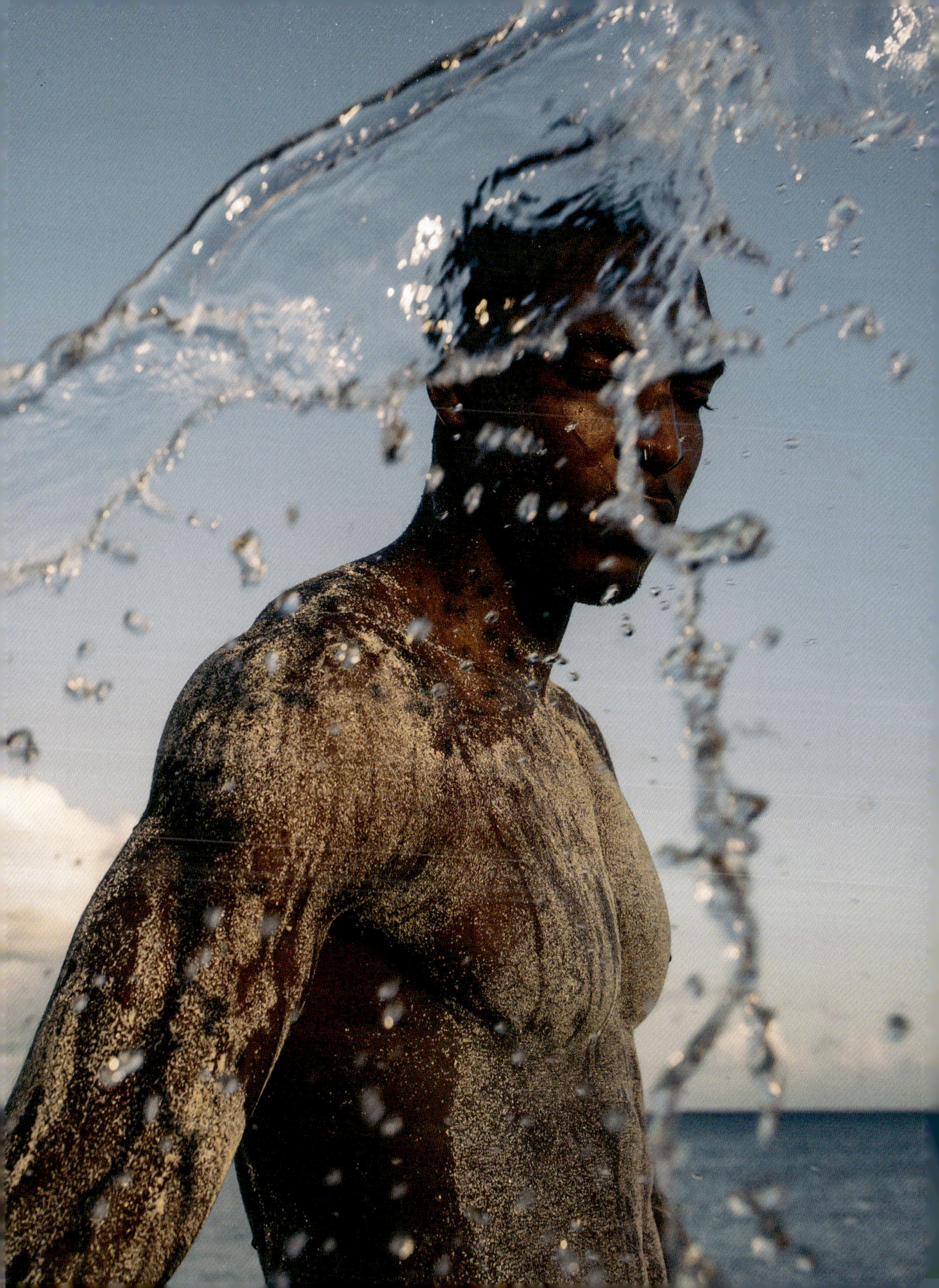

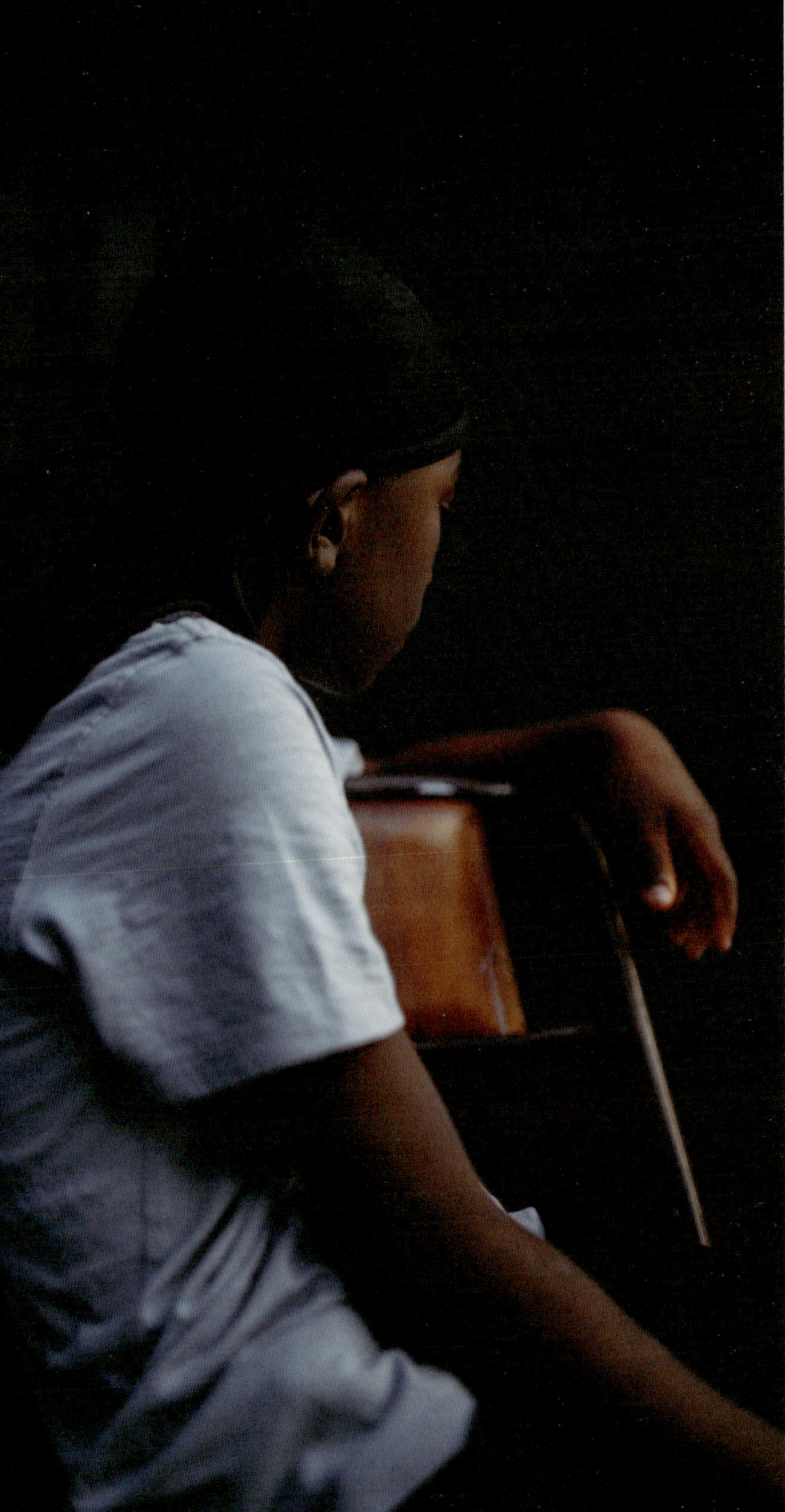

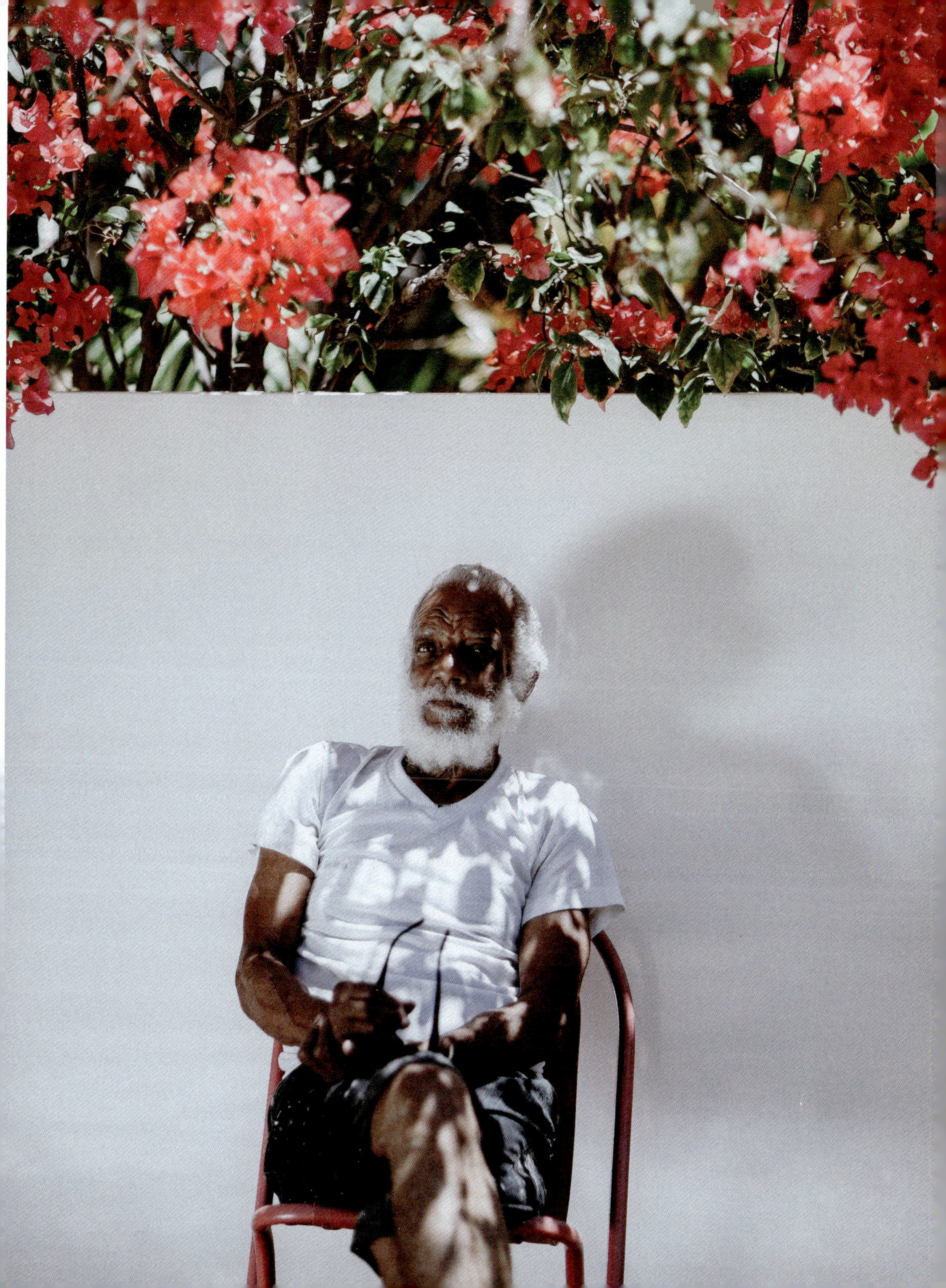